Dedicated to the memory of Isaac Asimov

The publisher would like to thank the following for permission to reproduce copyright material:

Photo and art credits:
Our Solar System:
Pp. 12, 13 (upper), 14–15, 15, 18, 142 (upper), © Tom Miller; p. 13 (lower), National Optical Astronomy Observatories; p. 17, © David Hardy; pp. 20, 24, © Lynette Cook, 1988; pp. 22, 29, © Lynette Cook, 1987; pp. 21, 23 (all), 27 (both), courtesy of NASA; p. 25, © Michael Carroll; p. 26 © Kurt Burmann, 1988; pp. 28–29 (upper), © Dennis Milon; p. 30 (upper), © George East; p. 30 (lower), © Julian Baum, 1988; p. 31 (both), © John Laborde; pp. 32–33 (upper), © Brian Sullivan, 1988; p. 33 (lower), © Doug McLeod; p. 34 Space Science Telescope Institute; p. 35 (upper), © John Foster; p. 35 (lower), © Paul DiMare; endsheets and p. 142 (lower), © Ron Miller.

Mercury: The Quick Planet:
P. 47, © Rick Sternbach; pp. 38, 44, 46, 49 (both), 59, 61 (right), photographs courtesy of NASA; p. 39, © Stan Christensen, courtesy of Beloit Corporation; p. 40, © Pat Rawlings, 1988; p. 41, ©Julian Baum, 1988; p. 42, © Dorothy Sigler Norton; p. 43 ©Lynette Cook, 1988; p. 45 (full page), Jet Propulsion Laboratory; front cover and p. 45 (inset), © Larry Ortiz; p. 48, courtesy of NASA; pp. 50–51, © David A. Hardy; p. 51 (upper left), © MariLynn Flynn, 1987; p. 51 (upper right), © Garret Moore, 1986; p. 52 (both), © Richard Baum, 1988; p. 53, courtesy of New Mexico State University Observatory; p. 54, © Dennis Milon; pp. 55, 58 (upper), A.I.P. Niels Bohr Library; p. 56 (upper), The Moshe ben Shimon Collection; pp. 56–57 (lower), Matthew Groshek, © Gareth Stevens, Inc.; pp. 57, 58 (lower), © Keith Ward, 1988; p. 60, © Pamela Lee; p. 61 (center), The University of Chicago Library; p. 144 (inset), © Sally Bensusen, 1988; pp. 144–145, © Sally Bensusen, 1987.

Venus: A Shrouded Mystery:
P. 64, photograph by William P. Sterne, Jr., Tulsa, Oklahoma; p. 65, © Keith Ward, 1990; pp. 66–67 (lower), photographs courtesy of New Mexico State University Observatory; p. 68 (full page), photograph courtesy of Crisp, Sinton, Ragent, Hodapp, 1989; pp. 68 (inset), 69 observations of the transit of Venus, 9 December, 1874, from the collection of Yerkes Observatory; pp. 70, 74–75 (background), 76 (full page), © MariLynn Flynn, 1987; pp. 71 (upper, both), 73 (upper), 83, 86 (full page), courtesy of NASA; p. 71 (lower), ©MariLynn Flynn, 1990; p. 72, © Paul DiMare, 1990; p. 73 (lower), photograph courtesy of the Naval Research Laboratory; p. 74 (inset, upper), © David Hardy; p. 74–75 (inset, lower), ©Sovfoto; p. 76 (inset), Matthew Groshek, 1980; p. 77, © Julian Baum, 1990; p. 78 (full page), © Garret Moore, 1990; p. 78 (inset), ©Rick Karpinski/DeWalt and Associates, 1990; p. 79 (upper), from the collection of the Yerkes Observatory; p. 79 (lower), courtesy of Richard Baum; p. 80, illustration courtesy of NASA; p. 81, Jet Propulsion Laboratory; p. 82 (both), courtesy of the United States Geological Survey; front cover and p. 84, © Mark Maxwell, 1990; p. 85, © Richard Baum, 1990; p. 86 (inset), © Garret Moore, 1989; p. 87, courtesy of Mitchell Park Conservatory; p. 146 (inset), © Thomas O. Miller/Studio "X"; pp. 146–147 (upper spread), © Sally Bensusen.

Earth: Our Home Base:
Front cover and pp. 104 (both), 105 (lower right), 106, courtesy of NASA; pp. 90–91 (both), 92 (upper), © John Foster, 1988; p. 92 (lower), © William Hartmann; p. 93 (upper right), Lick Observatory; pp. 93 (left), 102–103 (lower), 109 (upper), © Lynette Cook, 1988; pp. 94, 96, © Julian Baum, 1988; pp. 95 (upper), p. 105 (upper), United States Geological Survey; pp. 95 (lower), 99 (lower), 100 (upper), © Garret Moore, 1988; p. 97 (upper), photo by: R.E. Wallace/USGS; p. 97 (upper left), photo by: T. L. Youd/USGS; p. 97 (lower right), photo by: R. Kachadoorian/USGS; pp. 98–99 (upper), photo by: K. Segerstrum/USGS; p. 99 (upper left), photo by: J.D. Griggs/USGS; p. 99 (middle left), photo by: D.W. Peterson/USGS; p. 99 (middle right), photo by: P.W. Lipman/USGS; p. 100 (lower), © Mark Maxwell, 1988; p. 101 (both), National Severe Storms Laboratory; p. 103 (upper left and right), © Forrest Baldwin; p. 105 (middle), Jet Propulsion Laboratory; p. 107 (upper left), © Tom Miller; p. 107 (upper right), © Chappell Studio; p. 107 (lower), © Brian Parker/Tom Stack and Associates; p. 108 (upper), © Gary Milburn/Tom Stack and Associates; p. 108 (all lower, including diagram), © Center for Environmental Education; p. 109 (lower left and lower right), © Rain Forest Action Network; pp. 110, 111, © Doug McLeod, 1988; p. 112, © Pat Rawlings; p. 113, © David Hardy, 1988; pp. 148–149, 149 (lower), © Sally Bensusen, 1988.

Mars: Our Mysterious Neighbor:
P. 132, © Doug McLeod, 1987; pp. 116, 117 (upper), 136 (left), United States Geological Survey; pp. 117 (lower), 126–127 (upper), National Space Science Data Center; p. 118, Lowell Observatory; pp. 119 (upper), 120, 122–123 (upper), 129 (upper), Jet Propulsion Laboratory; pp. 119 (lower), 121, 123 (lower), 124, 125 (upper), 126 (lower), 127 (lower), 128, courtesy of NASA; back cover and p. 122 (lower), © John Foster, 1988; p. 125 (lower), © John Waite, 1987; p. 138, © Michael Carroll, 1985; pp. 129 (lower), 136 (right), © Michael Carroll, 1987; p. 130, © Kurt Burmann, 1986; p. 131 (upper), © Kurt Burmann, 1987; pp. 131 (lower), 139, © Julian Baum, 1988; p. 133 (upper), © David Hardy; p. 134, © Paul DiMare, 1985; p. 135 (upper), © MariLynn Flynn, 1985; pp. 133 (lower), 137, © MariLynn Flynn, 1987; p. 135 (lower), © Ron Miller, 1987; pp. 150–151, © Sally Bensusen, 1987.

Isaac Asimov's
THE ROCKY PLANETS

Modern Publishing
A Division of Unisystems, Inc.
New York, New York 10022
Printed in Italy

Contents

Introduction

The Universe we live in is an enormously large place. Only in the last 50 years or so have we learned how large it really is.

It's only natural that we would want to understand the place we live in, so in the last 50 years we have developed new instruments to help us learn about it. We have probes, satellites, radio telescopes, and many other things that tell us about the Universe.

Nowadays, human beings have walked on the Moon. We have seen planets up close. We have mapped Venus through its clouds. We have seen dead volcanoes on Mars and live ones on Io, one of Jupiter's satellites.

Let's take a look at our Solar system!

Isaac Asimov

The worlds we have seen up close, so far, are all members of the Sun's family. They are worlds that orbit the Sun, as the Earth does. We call the whole the Solar system, because "Sol" is the Latin word for "Sun" and the Sun is the center object of the system and by far its largest. The worlds of the Solar system are quite different from each other, and each is, in its own way, a fascinating place. *Isaac Asimov*

OUR SOLAR SYSTEM

The Beginnings of Our Sun

Our Solar system — the Sun and its family of planets — has not always existed.

Imagine this: It is nearly five billion years ago, and there is no Solar system — no planets, no moons, no Sun. Instead, there is a vast cloud of dust and gas called a nebula. This cloud has been slowly swirling for perhaps 10 billion years, held together by its own gravity. Then, nearby, a star explodes. A supernova! The blast pushes the gases of our nebula together. That strengthens the gravitational pull of those gases even more, and they begin to come together still more. The whole cloud begins to contract, and as it does so, it swirls faster and faster, and grows smaller and smaller.

Nebula: a hotbed of glowing gases ripe for star formation. In this illustration, stars have begun to form out of the vast cloud of gas and dust.

© Tom Miller

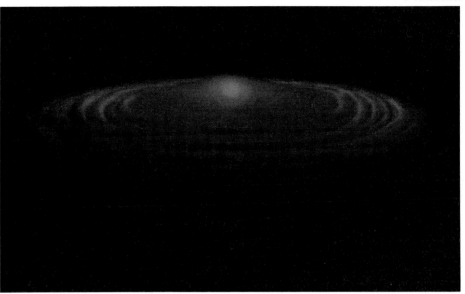

Our Sun as a "protostar": The cloud of gas and dust has begun to contract into a Solar nebula. At the center is a huge ball of glowing gases. This ball will eventually explode into life as our Sun. Here, however, it is a protostar, an early form of our Sun.

The Eagle Nebula is a spectacular sight. It is made up of both brightly glowing gas clouds and darker clouds of dust and gas that show up as black spots in this photograph.

The Birth of Our Sun

Let's look more closely at "our" nebula, the cloud we think started our Solar system.

The material of this nebula was more than 99% hydrogen and helium, the two simplest elements. These elements were formed at the very beginning of the Universe. Heavier elements made up the rest — less than 1%! These heavier elements had formed during the lives and explosive deaths of stars that were much larger than our Sun. These explosions spread the heavier elements through space.

As the nebula shrank, most of the material fell to the center and gathered into a huge ball of gas. At the center of this ball, matter became very hot and tightly packed. In this heat and pressure, hydrogen atoms collided and combined with each other to form helium.

This process is called nuclear fusion. The fusion released huge amounts of energy, and as this energy spread to the outer layers of the ball, it began to glow.

A star — our Sun — was born!

© Tom Miller

The Solar system as a pizza — of sorts.

Left: The Solar nebula, with the glowing young Sun at its center, continues to contract. The young planets are now clearly visible within the swirling disk.

Below: This diagram shows the paths of the early inner planets as they continue to capture material and grow.

© Tom Miller

Our Solar system: a cosmic pizza with everything — to go!

All the planets move about the Sun in the same direction. They all have orbits that are not very different from circles. They all move in almost the same plane. By that, we mean that if you built an exact model of the Solar system with all the planetary orbits marked out by curved wires, you could fit the whole thing into the kind of box that pizzas come in! When scientists worked out how the Solar system began, they had to figure out how it got to be this evenly spread out. In fact, the Solar system's pizza-like shape helped lead them to the idea of a contracting and rapidly swirling cloud of dust and gas.

Building the Planets

Away from the center of the cloud, the dust and gas were thinner. This material collected into a disk of hot gases. As the gases cooled, tiny particles began to form. Nearer the center, only rocky elements could become solid particles. Farther from the Sun, icy material could form from the cooling gas. These particles began to collide and stick together, forming larger clumps. Some clumps grew more quickly than others, and their increased mass gave them greater gravity, allowing them to gather more material and grow even more quickly. The rocky planets Mercury, Venus, Earth, and Mars formed where the temperatures were high. The gas giants formed farther away from the heat of the Sun.

Meanwhile, the energy created at the center of the Sun was beginning to reach the surface of our star and radiate into space, along with a "wind" of energetic particles. This radiation and solar wind began to push out the remaining dust and gas of the nebula, sweeping the Solar system clean.

Opposite: An artist's conception of how the Solar system came into its own.

1 (upper picture): "Protoplanets," youthful planets and moons forming out of the Solar nebula that was our early Solar system.

2 (middle): The great "wind" of energy from the young Sun "blowing away" remaining nebular matter, leaving most of the solid particles — and the Sun — that make up the Solar system as we know it today.

3 (lower): Our Solar system today. The view is from beyond the planet Jupiter.

© Tom Miller 1988

This diagram shows our Sun and its family of planets, from
the innermost outward: Mercury, Venus, Earth, Mars, Jupiter,
Saturn, Uranus, Neptune, and Pluto. Also shown is the Solar
system's "ecosphere." This is the area around the Sun that
is neither too hot nor too cold for life to exist, as long as
other conditions — such as an atmosphere — are suitable
for life. In this picture, only Venus, Earth, and Mars are in
the ecosphere, which is shown as red. And of these planets,
Venus is quite close to the hot zone (yellow), and Mars is too
close to the cold zone (blue). Earth is close to the center of
the ecosphere, where the temperatures seem best suited for
supporting life forms as we know them.

The Sun's Family

As we know, the Sun is by far the largest member of its Solar system family. In fact, it weighs about 500 times as much as everything else in the Solar system put together! It is the only object large enough for its center to undergo nuclear fusion, and so it produces so much energy that it shines. The planets are all much smaller, and nuclear fusion cannot occur at their centers. Their centers are warm, but they are cold on the surface. They only shine by reflecting light from the Sun.

In addition to the larger planets, there are many smaller bodies. Most of them circle the Sun as the planets do, but a few circle the planets themselves as natural satellites, or moons.

Let's take a closer look at the planets.

A companion star? Why not?

Most stars have companions, so they are called double stars. Our own nearest neighbor, Alpha Centauri, is a triple-star system. As far as we know, our Sun is a single star. We know for sure there is no other <u>bright</u> star near it. But what about a <u>dim</u> star? Could there be a tiny companion of the Sun? Some astronomers have recently suggested that there might be one, looking just like an ordinary dim star, and we just haven't noticed it yet!

A cutaway view of Mars showing the structure of a typical rocky planet. The thickness of the crust is like of the skin of an apple compared to the rest of the apple: It's quite thin!

Mercury, Venus, Earth, Mars — The Rocky Planets

The planets that formed quite near the Sun grew very warm because of all its heat. Hot gases, especially if they are light, are harder to hold by gravitational pull than cold gases. The nearby planets could not hold the very light hydrogen and helium that made up most of the swirling material. They could only hold onto the small amount of matter that made up heavier gases, metal, and rock. The nearby planets are therefore much smaller than the planets that formed farther away from the Sun. The nearby planets are mostly rock with metal at the center. They are thus called the "rocky planets," and our own Earth is one of them.

The rocky planets are actually quite small compared to the planets that formed farther away from the Sun. On the left (top to bottom) are Earth and Venus. Just to the right of Earth are Mars, Mercury, and Earth's Moon. Immediately below are Io and Europa (both moons of Jupiter). Below them are Ganymede and Callisto, also moons of Jupiter; and below them is Titan, Saturn's largest moon. Callisto is about the same size as the planet Mercury, and Ganymede and Titan are actually larger than Mercury. All three moons are only slightly smaller than Mars. Io is slightly larger, and Europa is slightly smaller, than our Moon.

NASA

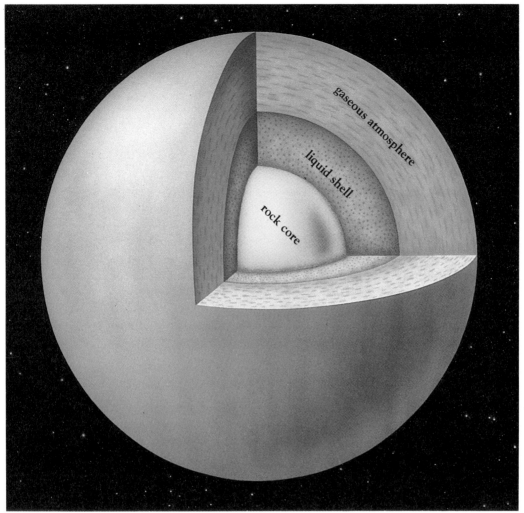

Cutaway of a gas giant: Uranus. Its core is made of rock.
Above the core is a "sea" made mostly of water, ammonia,
and methane, and a gaseous atmosphere made up mostly
of hydrogen.

© Lynette Cook 1987

Jupiter, Saturn, Uranus, Neptune — The Gas Giants

The planets that formed farther from the Sun were much cooler than the nearer planets. The hydrogen and helium gases were therefore cold enough for the planets to hold them with their gravitation. That meant they grew still larger and had even stronger gravitational pulls that could attract still more gas. The outer planets thus grew much larger than the inner ones. Instead of being rock and metal, they are made up mostly of the two gases, hydrogen and helium. For that reason, and because they are so large, they are called gas giants.

The gas giants, clockwise from right: Jupiter (photo), Saturn (photo), Uranus (painting), Neptune (painting).

NASA

NASA

NASA

NASA

23

Pluto, a little ball of ice on the fringes of our
Solar system.

Pluto — The Tiny Planet

The farthest planet we can see is not a gas giant. It is an oddball
little planet called Pluto. Pluto is even smaller than the inner
planets. It was the last planet to be discovered, and the dimmest.
It has a very lopsided orbit, so that at one end it even comes in a
little closer to the Sun than does Neptune, the next inner planet.
Pluto's orbit is tilted, though, and there's no chance of a collision
with Neptune. In the last few years we have found out that Pluto
is made up not of rock, and not of gases, but of ice — quantities of
water and other similar substances all frozen in the terrible cold so
far from our Sun.

What next — a tenth planet?

About 70 years ago, it seemed to astronomers that the outermost planets didn't move quite as they ought to. Perhaps there was a ninth planet out beyond Neptune, and perhaps its gravitational pull was making the outermost planets behave oddly. They searched for many years and finally found Pluto in 1930. That seemed to settle everything. But then, as more years passed, it turned out that Pluto was so small, its gravitational pull couldn't possibly affect the outermost planets. Does that mean there is another planet beyond Neptune — a large one? We don't know.

Planet X. Is it our tenth planet? We think it might be out there, beyond Pluto, tugging away at the outermost planets of our Solar system. But if there is such a thing as Planet X, it would be so far away and so faint that it would be hard to detect.

© Michael Carroll

25

Satellites — Little Worlds that Circle the Planets

When the planets grew, some of the material on the outskirts remained separate. All of the gas giants have little worlds, or satellites, that orbit them. Jupiter, the largest planet, has four rather large satellites and many smaller ones. Saturn has one large satellite and a number of middle-sized and small ones. Uranus has a number of middle-sized and small ones, but Neptune has only one large one and one small one. Even little Pluto has a small satellite of its own. The rocky planets are not so rich in satellites. Mars has two tiny ones, while Mercury and Venus have none at all. Our Earth has a large satellite — our Moon.

A study in contrasts: the Red Planet — Mars — and its dark little moon — Deimos. Don't let this imaginary view from Deimos fool you. Mars is close to 4,000 miles (6,400 km) wide, while Deimos is only 6-10 miles (10-16 km) wide.

© Kurt Burmann 1988

Left: Jupiter and its planet-sized moons, as photographed by the Voyager 1 probe. They are shown here not according to size but in their correct positions. Reddish Io (upper left) is closest to Jupiter (upper right). Next farthest out is Europa (center), followed by Ganymede (lower left) and Callisto.

Below: Photos of six of the Solar system's largest satellites, shown as they compare in size. Our Moon (center) is surrounded (clockwise from lower right) by Saturn's Titan and Jupiter's Callisto, Io, Europa, and Ganymede.

NASA

NASA

The journey of the Solar system

The Moon goes around the Earth, and the Earth goes around the Sun — but the Sun doesn't stand still, either. The Sun, carrying the entire Solar system with it, is moving steadily around the center of our Galaxy. All the other stars of the Galaxy are doing it, too, so that the whole Galaxy is constantly swirling. It takes our Solar system 200 million years to make one circle about the Galaxy. That means that since the Solar system was formed, nearly five billion years ago, it has circled the Galaxy 23 times.

A time-exposure photo of the Leonid meteor shower taken from Kitt Peak, Arizona, on November 17, 1966. The meteors show up as pinkish streaks that seem to be heading straight for Earth, while the stars make slightly curved trails across the early morning sky. The Leonid showers occur every year, but they are especially heavy every 33 years. The next heavy occurrence should be in 1999.

Cosmic Debris — Asteroids and Meteors . . .

Some of the material in the outskirts of the original cloud did not form large planets but stayed small. This is especially so between the orbits of Mars and Jupiter. There may be as many as 100,000 small bodies called asteroids that are at least a mile across and circle the Sun. A few have been captured by planets and have become small satellites. Some move in closer to the Sun and even pass near Earth. We know them as <u>meteoroids</u> while they are in space, <u>meteors</u> as they enter Earth's atmosphere in a fiery blaze, and <u>meteorites</u> when they actually hit Earth's surface. Very tiny ones might hit our astronauts or rockets out in space, and every once in a while one may hit the Earth.

Planning a trip to another sun?

Before you do, you should have some numbers handy! As you might know, the planets are spread out over great distances. Earth is about 93 million miles (150 million km) from the Sun, but the outer planets are much farther still. The average distance of Pluto from the Sun is about 3.6 billion miles (5.8 billion km). It is about 40 times as far from the Sun as Earth is. There is, however, plenty of room for the Solar system to spread out. Beyond it there are no other stars for trillions of miles. The very nearest star system, Alpha Centauri, is about 7,000 times as far away from us as Pluto is — about 25 trillion miles (40 trillion km)!

Below: a diagram highlighting the asteroid belt between Mars and Jupiter. Also shown are the paths of some of the oddball asteroids that orbit the Sun at crazy angles, as well as the Trojan asteroids — an army of asteroids that "lead" and "follow" Jupiter in its path around the Sun. This diagram also shows Jupiter's thin ring, revealed for the first time by Voyager 1 in 1979.

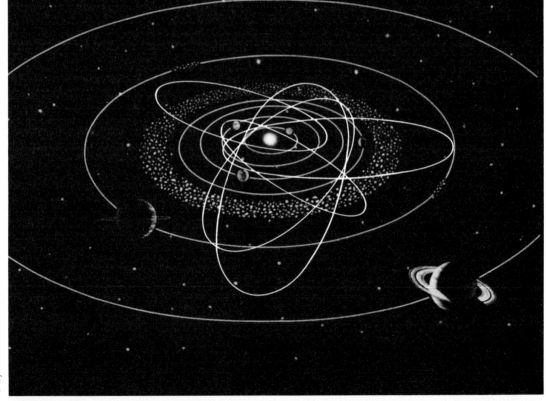

. . . and More Cosmic Debris — Comets

There's far more to our Solar system than meets the eye! Far beyond Pluto there may be a hundred billion small lumps of ice left over when the cloud of dust and gas contracted to form the Solar system. We call these lumps comets. Every once in a while something happens that causes one of them to drop toward the Sun and pass by the planets. The comet-ice evaporates in the Sun's heat. Clouds of trapped dust emerge and surround the comet, glittering in the sunlight. Solar wind, which is made of energetic particles shot out by the Sun, sweeps the dust around the comet into a luminous tail. This tail always points away from the Sun, and that can give us a magnificent view of the comet from Earth.

© George East

© Julian Baum 1988

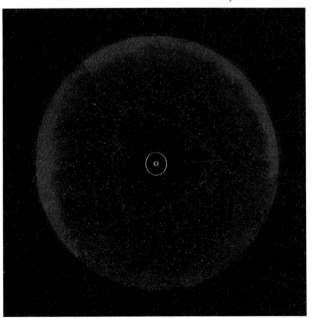

Above: Comet West. Everyone dreams of seeing a comet like this streaking across the sky. But to get such a spectacular view — and photo — you'd have to be far away from city lights.

Left: an artist's conception of a vast cloud of comets (red) enveloping our Solar system (yellow). Astronomers have studied the orbits of comets and concluded that there is such a huge cloud containing hundreds of billions of comets. This cloud lies thousands of times farther from the Sun than Pluto. The cloud is called the Oort cloud after Jan Oort, the astronomer who first suggested its existence in 1950.

These two photos show the movement of Comet Kobayashi-Berger-Milon 1975h across the sky in one day.

Left: A spiral galaxy (lower right part of picture) appears to lie just off the comet's path.

Below: The same spiral galaxy (upper right part of picture) shows the comet's progress. Also visible in this picture are the "streamers" in the comet's gas tail.

The End of the Solar System

Our Solar system works just fine, with the Sun and all its planets, moons, asteroids, and comets revolving and rotating like a wonderful machine. But it won't last forever. The hydrogen at the Sun's center will run low. After another five billion years, that will cause changes to take place at the center and the Sun will expand and become huge. The outer layers will cool and redden, turning the Sun into a red giant. The total heat, though, will be enough to burn Earth to a cinder, and all life upon it will be destroyed. Finally, the Sun will not be able to have any kind of nuclear fusion at its center. It will collapse into a tiny white dwarf no bigger than the Earth, with cold, dead planets circling it.

What will life be like on our planet just before this happens? Will human beings even be around? Your guess is as good as anyone's.

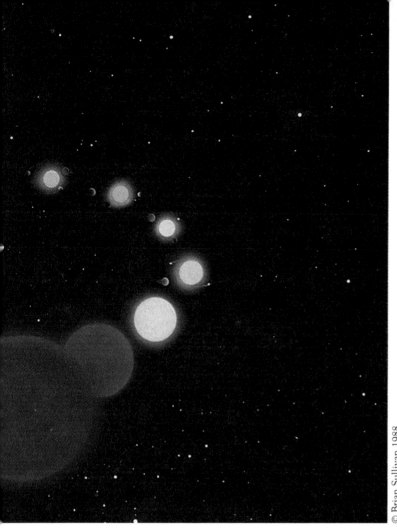

The life and death of a star.

This picture shows a star like our Sun passing through its life. From the nebula at far left, a cloud of gas and dust contracts into a Solar nebula. The protosun and disk (rear center) take on the shape of our Sun and Solar system as we know them today (upper right). Billions of years from now, as the Sun loses energy, it will expand outward (far center-right), eventually becoming a red giant (lower right). Finally, its store of nuclear energy will be completely used up. It will collapse into a white dwarf (front center) no bigger than Earth, and Earth itself will be little more than a dead, burned-up cinder.

There is a small white star in Earth's future. Imagine our Earth, and us on it, somewhere in time between the Sun as we know it now (bottom) and the tiny white dwarf that it will someday become (top).

Other Solar Systems?

It doesn't seem likely that our Sun is the only star to have a family of planets. There are hundreds of billions of stars in our Galaxy, and hundreds of billions of other galaxies. And in each of those galaxies, every star is itself a sun. Some scientists think that most or even all of these stars have planets. The trouble is that even the nearest stars are so far away, we can't detect any planets that may exist. In the last few years we have found that some stars seem to be circled by clouds of small bits of matter. Planets may be among them. In fact, in 1987 astronomers in Hawaii made an exciting discovery: a large body that seems to be orbiting a nearby star. Perhaps some day, with improved instruments, we will see just what's out there.

This is a false color photo of the star Beta Pictoris. The star itself has been blocked out so its bright light would not interfere with the picture of a disk stretching out beyond the star. Astronomers think that this disk might be a solar system or early solar system. This would mean that there are, as many suspect, other planetary systems out there — an exciting thought.

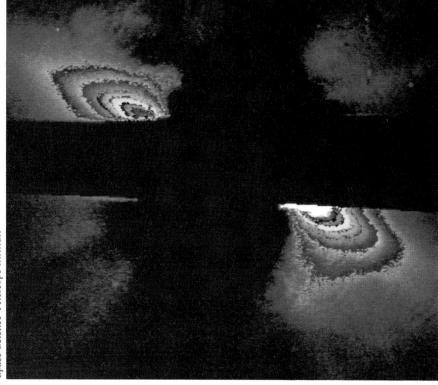

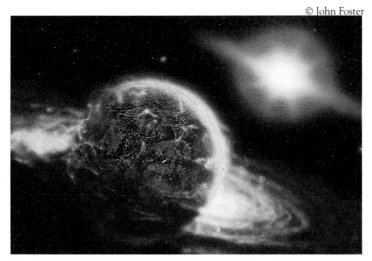

© John Foster

© Paul DiMare

Two imaginary views of planets in other parts of the Universe. Above: planets forming in a young solar system.

Right: two desolate planets in a distant solar system. Beyond them is a stellar treat that is rare but actually exists — a "polar-ring" galaxy with a vast band of stellar matter actually encircling the galaxy itself.

Clouds of comets — stepping stones to the stars?

Astronomers have never seen the Oort cloud — the cloud of comets supposed to exist far beyond the planets. But astronomers have reasons to think the comets are there. If they are there, it is possible they extend outward for over 10,000 billion miles (16,000 billion km), or nearly halfway to the nearest star (Alpha Centauri). Does Alpha Centauri also have a cloud of comets reaching out toward us? It is interesting to imagine comets all the way across between ourselves and Alpha Centauri — kind of a bridge between us and our nearest stellar neighbor.

One of the planets we have seen up close is Mercury, which is the nearest planet to the Sun. It is so near the Sun that it is usually overwhelmed by the Sun's light when we try to see it. That is one reason why until recently we knew very little about Mercury. That is changed now. We have learned quite a bit, and in this chapter we will try to explain our new knowledge of this small, quick planet.

Isaac Asimov

MERCURY: The Quick Planet

The Silent Fire

Mercury is a small planet — at 3,030 miles (4,875 km) across, it is only three-eighths the width of Earth. It is the closest planet to the Sun — only 36 million miles (57.9 million km) away on the average. And it comes as close as 29 million miles (46.6 million km) as it orbits the Sun. This is almost 70% closer to the Sun than Earth is.

The surface of any planet this close to the Sun is bound to get very hot — as hot as 660°F (348°C), which is hot enough to melt lead. And since Mercury is so close to the Sun, the Sun's gravity pulls hard. Earth moves about the Sun at 18.6 miles (29.9 km) a second, but Mercury moves at an average of 29.8 miles (47.9 km) a second. It is the quick planet.

Opposite: the planet Mercury as seen by the Mariner 10 spacecraft in 1974. Its rough, cratered surface resembles that of our Moon.

Right: Glowing streams of molten metal pour into molds at a foundry. The surface of Mercury gets hot enough to melt lead.

The Two-year Day and Other Orbital Oddities

From our point of view here on Earth, Mercury has a strange relationship with the Sun. First of all, its closeness to the Sun gives it a small orbit. It moves so quickly that its trip around the Sun — its year — takes only 88 days. But Mercury turns very slowly on its <u>axis</u>, so the time from sunrise to sunrise — one Mercury day — is 176 Earth days. So Mercury's "day" is twice as long as its year!

Mercury turns on its axis with a steady speed, but its orbit is lopsided, and when it is nearer the Sun it moves faster. For that reason, the Sun moves across Mercury's sky unevenly. In fact, from certain places on Mercury, you might see the Sun rise, then set (as though it had changed its mind), and then rise again! The same would go for sunset, too — first the Sun would set, then rise briefly, and then set again.

Opposite: daytime on Mercury. Space suits would have to withstand extreme heat and cold on a planet bathed in bright sunlight and deep shadows.

Below: In this illustration, the bright yellow area of Mercury's tipped, lopsided orbit lies <u>above</u> Earth's orbital plane (shown in blue). The pink area lies <u>below</u> Earth's orbital plane. A red line shows the 7° tilt between the two orbital planes.

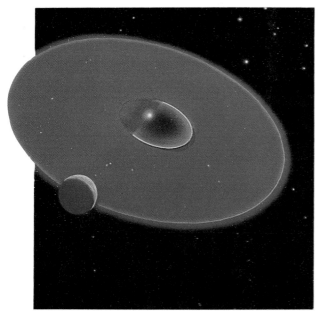

Mercury — why the wacky orbit?

Mercury's orbit is more elliptical, or lopsided, than any planetary orbit except Pluto's. Mercury's orbit is also more tipped against the general plane of planetary orbits than any orbit except Pluto's. Actually, since Mercury is so near the Sun, astronomers might think its orbit should be nearly circular and in the plane of the Sun's equator, like the orbit of Venus, the next closest planet to the Sun. Why isn't this so in Mercury's case? We don't know.

Mercury — The Inside Story

When the Solar system formed, the material outside the Sun formed vast crowds of small bodies. These small bodies gradually crashed into each other and formed larger bodies. The gravitational pull of the larger bodies attracted most remaining small bodies, and so the planets formed.

Very close to the Sun, the lighter material all boiled away. Mercury formed only out of rocks and metal — materials that have a very high melting point. Mercury is therefore second only to Earth in density. Like Venus and Earth, Mercury has a large metallic center. But of all the known planets in our Solar system, Mercury's metallic center seems to be the largest for its size.

Mercury's building blocks were rock and metal fragments that formed close to the Sun.

Beneath Mercury's Sun-baked surface lies a large central core of metal.

The negatives and positives of Mercury's magnetic field

Earth and at least three of the four giant planets have magnetic fields. To have a magnetic field, a planet must have a liquid center that conducts electricity, and it must rotate swiftly so that it sets the liquid swirling. The Moon and Mars do not have liquid centers, so they have no magnetic fields. Mercury rotates very slowly, so it shouldn't have a magnetic field. But it does. It has a weak magnetic field, and astronomers can't figure out why.

The Cooling Surface of a Hot Planet

When a world forms, the last few bits that strike it leave huge craters where they hit the surface. If the world is like Earth, its water and atmosphere wear down these craters and make most disappear. If the world has volcanic action, the lava from the volcanoes covers the surface and, again, most craters disappear.

Small worlds like Mercury usually don't have atmospheres or volcanic activity, so the marks left by the final collisions remain. We can see many craters on Earth's Moon, for example. Mercury, meanwhile, is so hot that its surface remained soft longer. It is even more thickly covered with craters than the Moon!

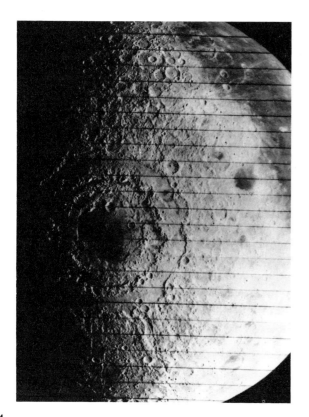

Left: Both Mercury and our Moon share the scars of collisions. The Moon's Mare Orientale impact site looks very much like a similar basin on Mercury. On the Moon, though, we can still see where lava flows later smoothed over the surface.

Opposite: Craters and bright "rays" of debris crowd Mercury's south polar area. Inset: an artist's concept of heavily cratered Mercury.

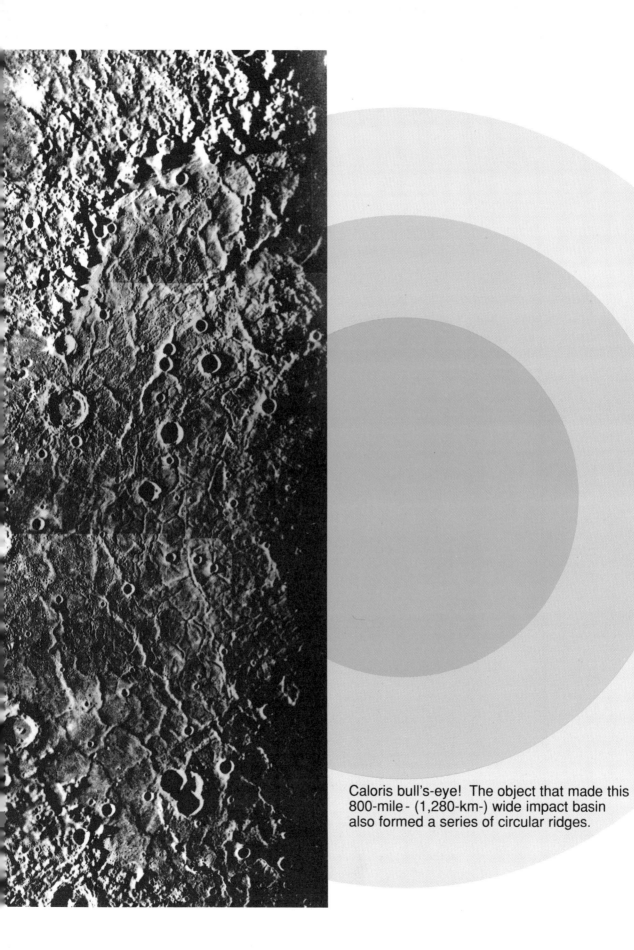

Caloris bull's-eye! The object that made this 800-mile- (1,280-km-) wide impact basin also formed a series of circular ridges.

Mercury — A Tortured Landscape

If we were to see Mercury as closely as we see the Moon, it would look very much like the Moon. It is thickly covered with craters that look somewhat smaller than those on the Moon. But that is only because Mercury is a larger body, so its craters look smaller by comparison.

We call Mercury's largest crater Caloris (meaning "heat") because it happens to have the highest temperatures on Mercury. Caloris is about 810 miles (1,300 km) across. There are also cliffs and fissures that pass right across the craters. This may be because Mercury shrank as it slowly cooled, and the surface of the planet cracked.

An artist imagines the Caloris impact.

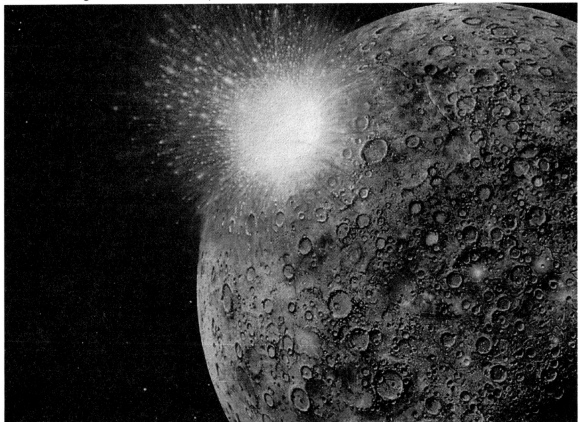

Mapping Mercury

Mercury has long been a mystery to Earthbound sky-watchers. In fact, until 1974, we didn't know anything about Mercury's surface. All we could see through a telescope was a small body near the Sun with vague shadows on it that went through phases, like the Moon and Venus.

But on November 3, 1973, scientists launched a space probe, Mariner 10, that would change our understanding of Mercury. Less than five months later — on March 29, 1974 — Mariner passed within 168.4 miles (271 km) of Mercury's surface. Then, as it went around the Sun, Mariner visited Mercury twice more, coming as close as 203 miles (327 km). It sent back detailed pictures of almost half of Mercury's surface.

Everything we know about the surface comes from those pictures. No other craft has been sent to Mercury since.

Opposite: Mariner 10 scanned Mercury's surface three times in 1974 and 1975, returning the pictures to Earth by radio beams.

Two views of Mercury. Left: the cracked floor of the Caloris basin. Right: a rugged, cratered landscape.

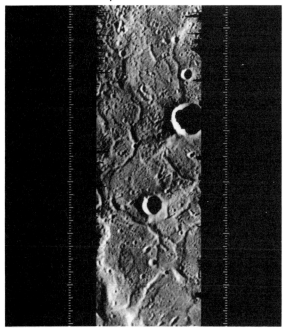
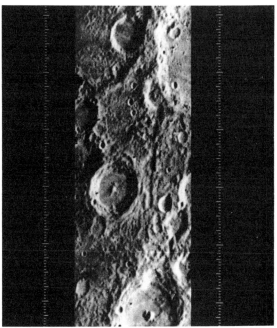

Piloted Missions to Mercury

Human beings have landed on the Moon, and plans are being made to send astronauts to Mars. But will we ever send human beings to Mercury? It might be useful to do this so we can study Mercury's surface up close.

But would it be possible to go to a planet with temperatures as hot as Mercury's? Perhaps. After all, any spot on Mercury is turned away from the Sun for 88 days at a time, so the temperature cools off rapidly. In fact, it actually gets very cold — as low as – 270°F (–168°C) — during Mercury's long night. So people with the right equipment might be able to remain on the surface during the night. But approaching the Sun to get to Mercury would be quite difficult — not just because of the heat, but because of the intense ultraviolet light, x-rays, and other radiation.

Sunrise on Mercury.

Left: Astronauts on Mercury examine surface rocks for useful minerals.

Below: Thick-walled buildings made from Mercury's rocks could protect human visitors from the Sun's deadly radiation.

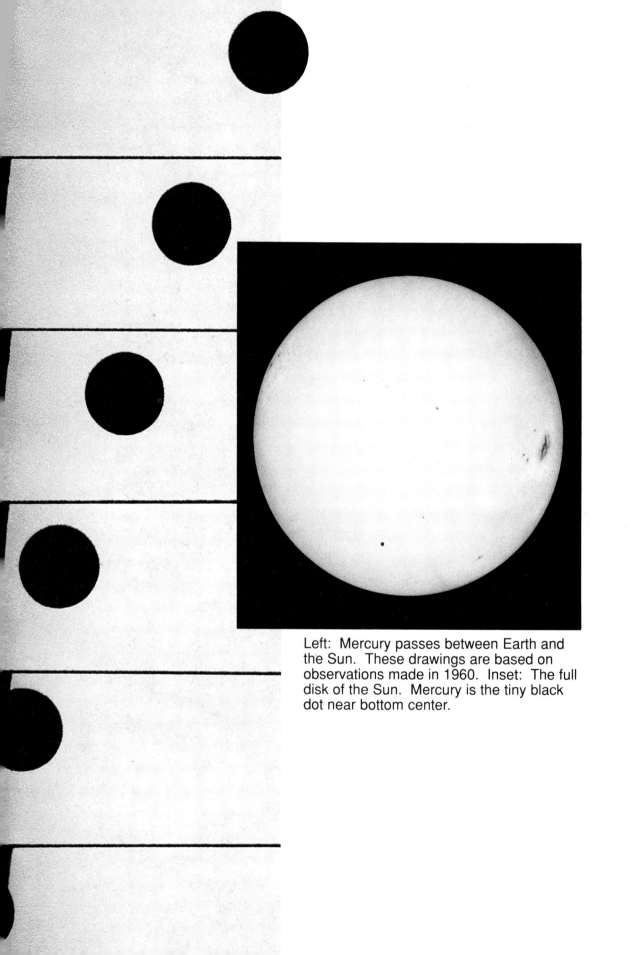

Left: Mercury passes between Earth and the Sun. These drawings are based on observations made in 1960. Inset: The full disk of the Sun. Mercury is the tiny black dot near bottom center.

Exploring Mercury from Earth

In earlier times, before spacecraft, we could only see Mercury from Earth as a bright, starlike object. Of the five planets (not counting Earth) that we can see without a telescope, Mercury was probably the last to be discovered. Even with a telescope, it looks small.

When Mercury is nearest Earth, the Sun is on the other side of it. During these times, Earth faces Mercury's nighttime surface. This means we can only see Mercury as a tiny dark disk as it crosses in front of, or transits, the surface of the Sun.

When Mercury is on the other side of the Sun, we <u>could</u> see its day side, except for one problem — the Sun hides it. We can only really see it well when it is to one side of the Sun. Then we see it as a tiny speck.

Our best views of Mercury from telescopes on Earth don't tell us much about the little planet. Even after the Sun sets, Mercury can only be seen through the thickest part of Earth's atmosphere, which blurs the image.

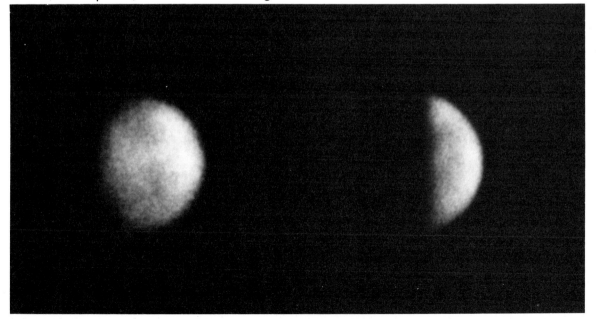

Searching for Mercury

Because Mercury is closer to the Sun than we are, we always see it quite close to the Sun. Most of the time, the Sun's glare makes it impossible to see Mercury. So we should look for it in the eastern sky just before sunrise, or in the western sky just after sunset.

In the evening, Mercury would be visible in the sky for just under an hour or so after the Sun sets. And in the dawn, Mercury would appear in the sky up to just under an hour before the Sun rises. Of course, by the time the Sun rises, our view of Mercury is wiped out.

So if you want to see Mercury, you have to search for it in the twilight or the dawn.

Opposite: Mercury and the crescent Moon. The entire disk of the Moon is dimly visible, illuminated by sunlight reflected from Earth.

Polish astronomer Nicolaus Copernicus, the man who argued that the planets circled around the Sun.

Looking for Mercury — to see or not to see?

Even around sunset or sunrise, Mercury is often so close to the Sun that it is hard to see. The sky is so bright just after sunset or just before sunrise that little Mercury can be missed. In 1543, Polish astronomer Nicolaus Copernicus explained that the planets circle the Sun, not Earth. Even Earth itself circles the Sun. He was one of the most famous astronomers ever, yet the story is that not once in his life did even he manage to catch sight of Mercury. ●

The Myth of Mercury —
The Gods' Quick Messenger

The planets are named after ancient gods. Mercury, the messenger of the ancient Roman gods, was usually shown with little wings on his helmet and on his sandals. These showed how rapidly he moved when he was carrying his messages. Because the planet Mercury moves across the sky more rapidly than the other planets, it was named for the speedy messenger of the gods.

Mercury on money. This 1942 US dime is called a Mercury dime. Actually, it shows the goddess of liberty wearing a winged helmet.

Metals were sometimes named for the planets, too. A certain metal looks like silver but is liquid. It was called quicksilver, which means "live silver." Quicksilver was also named for its "quickness" — so it was called "mercury." You've seen this kind of mercury in a thermometer. It's the silver liquid that shows the temperature of you or the world around you.

The metal mercury, or "quicksilver," forms shiny liquid drops at room temperature.

Mercury, messenger of the gods.

Quick Mercury —
fast and fooling the ancients

The ancients believed that the faster an object moves across the sky, the nearer to Earth it must be. The Moon moves faster than any other object, so it had to be closest to Earth. They were right about that. But Mercury moves faster than Venus does, so they thought Mercury was closer to Earth than Venus was. Today, we know that Mercury moves as fast as it does because it is near the Sun, not Earth. Venus is closer to Earth than Mercury is.

Albert Einstein, the physicist who explained Mercury's strange movements.

Could an unknown planet explain the odd motion of Mercury? Some astronomers went so far as naming this mystery world after Vulcan, the god of fire.

"Vulcan" — A Modern Myth of Mercury

Mercury moves in its orbit because it is held by the Sun's gravity. The other planets also pull on it slightly. But when all the gravitational pulls were calculated, it turned out that there was a tiny motion of Mercury that couldn't be explained.

Could this motion be caused by the pull of an undiscovered planet even closer to the Sun? For a time, people thought there might be such a planet, and it was called Vulcan, after the god of fire. In more than 50 years of looking, however, no one ever found this planet. Then scientist Albert Einstein worked out a new theory of gravity that accounted for Mercury's odd motion.

The need for a planet like Vulcan had vanished, and so, in the minds of many, did Vulcan!

A total solar eclipse darkened the area of space close to the Sun, giving astronomers a perfect chance — without success — to look for Vulcan.

Mercury's neighbors— getting an inside track on the Sun?

Some objects approach the Sun more closely than Mercury does. The asteroid Icarus comes to within about 17 million miles (28 million km) of the Sun, and some comets come even closer. If we could set up instruments near Mercury's poles, where the Sun is always near the horizon and it may not be <u>too</u> *hot, we could study these close approaches. We might even be able to study the Sun itself and get close-up answers to its many mysteries.* **?**

The Future — Our Key to Mercury's Past

One day, we will send spacecraft back to Mercury. After all, we have mapped less than half of its surface. There might be many interesting things to see on the rest of the Sun's nearest planetary neighbor.

We might like to know more about the cliffs on Mercury, and confirm our theory that they are caused by the planet's shrinking as it cooled off. We have no sign that other rocky worlds, like Venus or the Moon, have been shrinking. So Mercury would give us a chance to study what happens to a planet cooling off when it was formed close to the Sun. We would also like to know more about the interior of Mercury, and whether any quakes occur on Mercury.

Mercury may not be a planet that we would ever think of living on. It's just too close to the Sun. But it would be wonderful to explore more of the <u>inner</u> reaches of our Solar system, as well as its <u>outer</u> reaches. Mercury would be a perfect place to continue that search.

**Tiny Mercury —
small, but not a lightweight**

We used to think Mercury was the smallest planet. Now we know Pluto is even smaller. Even so, Mercury is smaller than some moons. Jupiter's largest moon, Ganymede, and Saturn's largest moon, Titan, are both larger than Mercury. But those moons seem to be made up mainly of icy material, while Mercury is made up of rock and metal. If you could put worlds on a scale, Mercury would weigh more than twice as much as either of those large, icy satellites.

As Mercury's interior cooled and shrank, the surface crust buckled and cracked. Above: an apple's skin wrinkles as the apple dries out and shrinks. Right: part of the fractured Caloris basin on Mercury.

Opposite: A robot lander of the future makes its first study of Mercury's soil.

The nearest of all planets to Earth,
Venus, has remained a mystery for
a long time. It has such a thick layer
of clouds that for years astronomers
could see nothing of its surface. They
couldn't tell how quickly it rotated or
even if it rotated at all. In this chapter,
we will tell you how much we have now
learned about this mysterious planet.

Isaac Asimov

VENUS: A Shrouded Mystery

Morning Star, Evening Star

Venus is the brightest of all the stars and planets in the sky. Only the Sun and the Moon are brighter. Unlike most planets, Venus never gets far away from the Sun in the sky, and so it can only be seen just before sunrise or just after sunset. When it is to the east of the Sun, Venus shines in the evening sky like a jewel and is called the Evening Star. When west of the Sun, it shines before dawn as the Morning Star.

The ancients thought the Morning Star and the Evening Star were two different objects. They even gave them different names before they noticed that these two "stars" could never be seen in the sky at the same time. Today we know that they are <u>one</u> object, not two.

Because of its lovely brightness, that object was named after the beautiful goddess of love, Venus.

Opposite: The Moon and Venus team up to form a spectacular duo in this multiple-exposure photograph of Tulsa, Oklahoma.

Right: Venus, the Roman goddess of love.

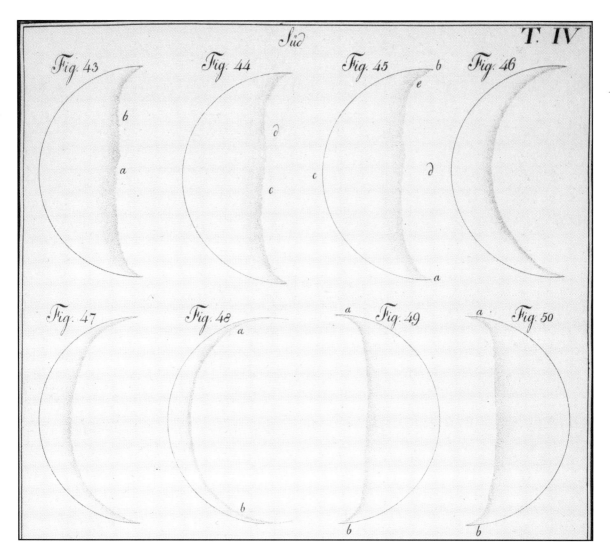

The phases of Venus as recorded by astronomers in the 18th century (above) and the 20th century (below).

Studying Venus

The ancient Babylonians noticed Venus's motion in the sky and became interested in the motions of the other planets, too. This encouraged the growth of astronomy, and of mathematics as well. Ptolemy (pronounced TOL-em-ee), an ancient Greek astronomer, worked out a way of predicting where Venus and the other planets would be at any given time. The only thing wrong was that he pictured Earth at the center of our Solar system, with the Sun and other planets revolving around it.

Italian astronomer Galileo Galilei was the first to use a telescope to view objects in the sky. In 1610, he studied Venus and found that it had phases, like Earth's Moon. Sometimes it was full, sometimes half-lit, sometimes just a crescent. By the old theory that everything went around Earth, Venus should have looked the same all the time. The fact that it changed helped prove that the planets, including Earth, went around the Sun.

Venus — one devil of a planet

The ancient Romans called the Morning Star Lucifer, *which means "bringer of light," for when the Morning Star rose, the Sun would follow. The king of Babylon was also called "the Morning Star." When the king was defeated in battle, the prophet Isaiah said, "How art thou fallen from heaven, O Lucifer, son of the morning!" Centuries later, people thought Isaiah was talking about the devil, cast out of heaven by God, so* Lucifer *became one of the names of Satan.*

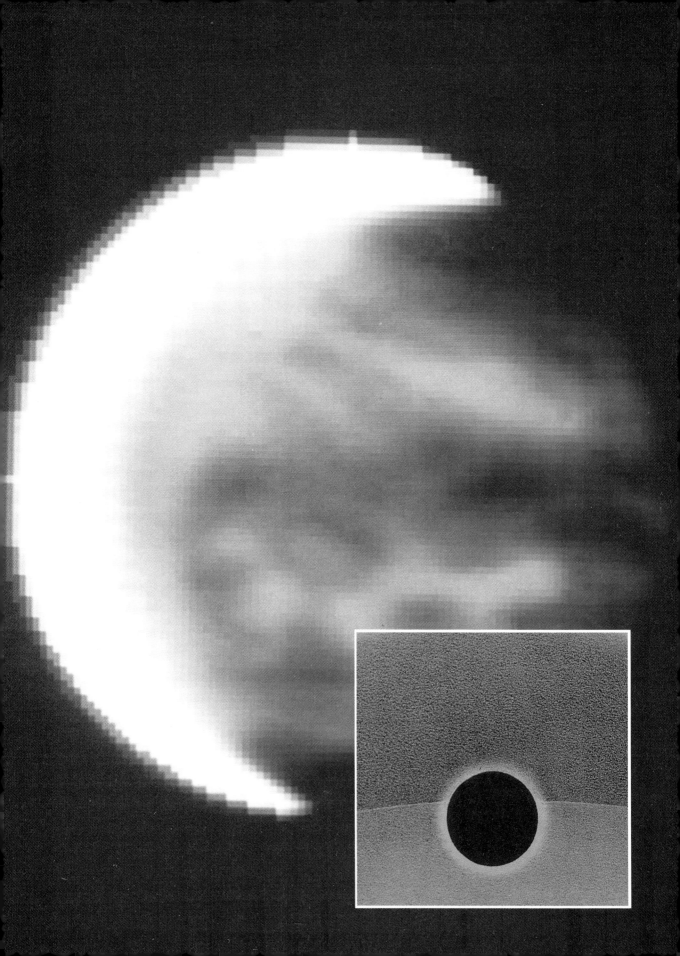

An Ocean of Clouds

When Venus is on the same side of the Sun as we are, it can be as close to Earth as 23.7 million miles (38.1 million km). This is closer than any other large object except for our own Moon. In 1761, a rare event called a solar transit occurred when Venus moved across the disk, or face, of the Sun. By watching this transit of Venus across the disk of the Sun, astronomers could tell that Venus had an atmosphere that contained clouds.

When we view Venus through a telescope, all we see are its yellowy clouds. For many years this thick cloud cover kept astronomers from learning much at all about Venus's surface — even though it is the planet closest to Earth.

Opposite (background): Heat-sensitive cameras reveal both the sunlit side of Venus (white) and warm clouds on the planet's night side (orange). Below and opposite (inset): The transit of Venus (black circle) in 1874 gave astronomers a chance to examine the planet's thick, cloudy atmosphere.

Venus — A Sister Planet?

The fact that Venus has such a thick layer of clouds made many people think it must have a lot of water on its surface. Venus is closer to the Sun than Earth is. While this means Venus gets more heat than we do, scientists thought Venus's clouds might reflect sunlight and keep the surface from getting too hot.

Some scientists, and many science fiction writers, pictured Mars as an old planet, looking like Earth might in the distant future. They also thought of Venus as a young planet, and imagined that it looked a lot like Earth in the prehistoric past, in the age of the dinosaurs. They pictured Venus as a tropical world with warm oceans and lots of plant and animal life. Since Venus is about the same size as Earth, many people looked upon it as Earth's twin.

In this artist's rendition, a distant volcano blasts a plume of dust and rock high above Venus's Asteria Regio region.

Left: Venus, so unlike Earth in many ways, is close in size to Earth — only about 5 percent smaller than our planet.

Below: Some pictured Venus as a swampy world much like prehistoric Earth.

The Temperature of Venus — Too Hot to Handle

In the 1950s astronomers began studying other kinds of radiation besides the tiny waves we see as light. All objects give off radiation — x-rays, radio waves, ultraviolet, infrared, and light. We can't see most radiation, but we can detect it with the right instruments. What's more, objects that are different temperatures give off different kinds of radiation. So by measuring what kind of radiation an object gives off and how much, astronomers can tell how hot it is.

In 1956, radio astronomers detected the radiation given off by Venus. They showed that Venus must be very hot — hotter than boiling water. Astronomers then knew that the cloud tops were hot. But they still couldn't tell what the temperature on the surface of the planet might be like.

Opposite: a cutaway view of Venus, showing how scientists believe the planet is put together. Like Earth, Venus probably has a hot core of liquid metal.

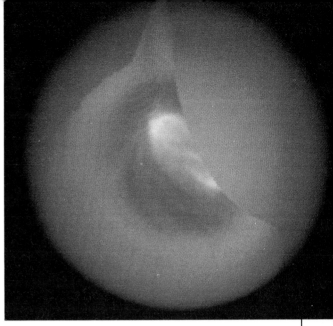

Above: A heat-sensitive camera aboard the Pioneer Venus probe shows the clouds above the north pole of Venus. A dense, crescent-shaped cloud bank spirals outward 10 miles (16 km) above the main cloud deck. The bright spots are probably caused by rapidly moving clouds clearing away to expose the warm atmospheric layers below.

Below: Radio telescopes helped scientists take the temperature of Venus.

In this artist's concept, a Russian Venera probe stands bathed in an eerie orange light on the surface of Venus.

A Nice Place to Visit, But...

There was only one way to find out more about Venus—go there. In 1961, the Soviet Union (now referred to as the Russian Federation) sent the first of 15 Venera probes to Venus. In 1967, Venera 4 actually decended into Venus' atmosphere and sent back information to Earth. In 1970, Venera 7 became the first probe to send back data from the planet's surface. Mariner 2, the first US probe to study the planet, flew past Venus in 1962. Its instruments showed that the surface of Venus was hot—about 890°F (477°C), hot enough to melt lead!

Venus's intense heat and incredible atmospheric pressure put the Venera probes out of action—but not before they sent back a wealth of information. We now know that Venus's atmosphere is so thick that standing on the planet would feel like being at the bottom of the ocean. We also know that the atmosphere of Venus is made up almost entirely of carbon dioxide, with no oxygen. The lightning-filled clouds also contain water mixed with sulfuric acid.

Background: An artist imagines lightning flashing in an orange Venusian sky. Below: The surface of Venus as photographed by Venera 13. The view includes the bottom of the lander.

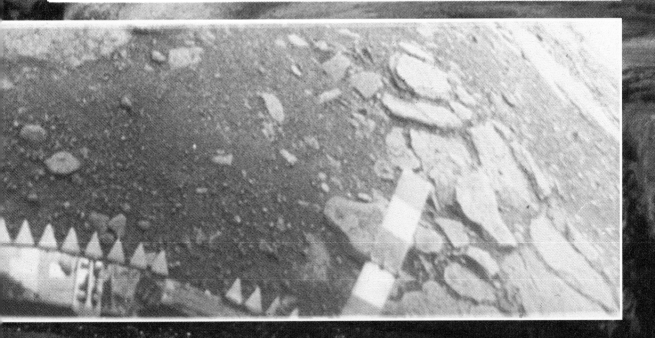

Earth's Twin or a Case of Mistaken Identity?

The probes all showed one thing — Venus is <u>not</u> a twin sister of Earth. Except for its size, it is completely different. Venus is far too hot to have oceans of water or any form of Earth-like life. Its surface is completely dry and desolate.

Venus's atmosphere is also completely unlike Earth's — in fact, it is almost the exact opposite. Venus's air is made up of 98 percent carbon dioxide and a little nitrogen. Earth's air is made up of 78 percent nitrogen, 21 percent oxygen, and less than 0.1 percent carbon dioxide.

The weather on Venus is strange by Earth's standards. Only one-sixth as much daylight gets through the clouds as we get here on Earth, so the light on Venus's surface is always dim. The pressure of Venus's atmosphere is 88 times that of Earth's. There is constant lightning up in the clouds. Acid rain falls from the sky but never reaches the ground. The blistering heat evaporates the drops before they land.

Opposite: an artist's rendering of hot gases jetting through a vent near one of Venus's volcanoes. Inset: Earth's serene beauty is unmatched anywhere in the Solar system — and certainly not on Venus!

Below: Venus as seen when nearest Earth.

Venus, the planet of 584 days — so what's in a number?

Venus moves around the Sun more quickly than Earth does. Every 584 days, Venus gains a lap on Earth. Also every 584 days, Venus is as close to Earth as it can get. Finally, Venus's rotation period is such that every 584 days it turns the same face to Earth. Surely that can't all be just coincidence. Some astronomers think Earth's gravity pulls at Venus and locks it into place. But Earth's gravity seems too weak for that. Could there be some other explanation?

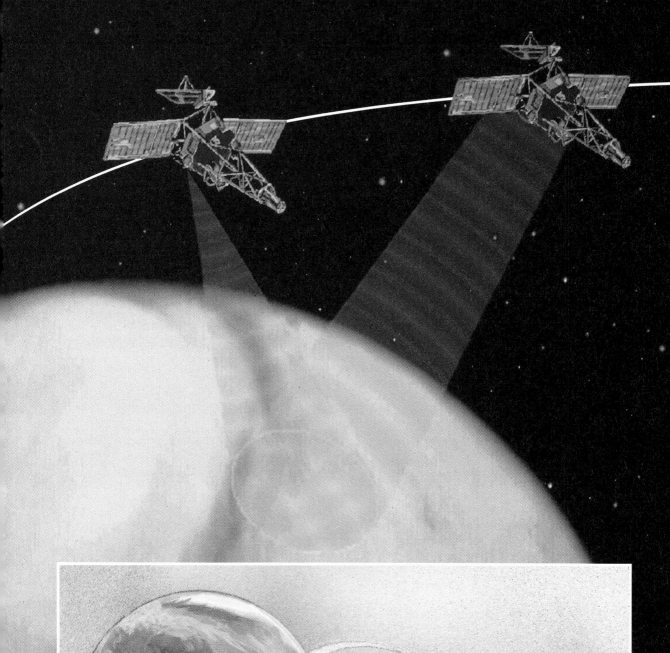

1
Venus Day =
243
Earth Days

The Backwards Planet?

Mariner 2 discovered other surprises about Venus as well. By sending radio waves through the clouds to the surface and then recording the echoes, the probe discovered that Venus rotates very slowly. It takes Venus 243 <u>days</u> to make one turn on its axis, while Earth takes just 24 <u>hours</u>.

What's more, Venus rotates in a direction exactly opposite that of Earth. Earth and most of the other planets turn counterclockwise, from west to east, but Venus turns clockwise, from east to west.

Famous astronomer E. C. Pickering estimated that Venus took only 21 hours to spin once on its axis.

Right: In 1951, R. M. Baum, an English astronomer observing Venus without the benefit of radio astronomy, determined the rotation of Venus to be 195 days.

Opposite (background): In this artist's concept, Mariner 2 determines Venus's rotation by bouncing radio waves off the planet's surface.

Opposite (inset): A more familiar version of the same procedure. At the rate of only one turn on its axis every 243 days, the planet Venus is not likely to receive a rotational speeding ticket!

Lost?
A compass won't help you here!

Venus, Mercury, and Earth all have
cores made up mostly of molten
iron. As the planet turns, the iron
swirls, setting up a magnetic field.
That is why Earth is a magnet and
why compasses work. But our
planet has to turn rapidly to make
the liquid center swirl sufficiently.
Venus has no magnetic field, so it
must turn too slowly. But Mercury
turns nearly as slowly as Venus
and _does_ have a magnetic field.
Why Mercury and not Venus?
It's a mystery.

?

The Mapmaker Probes

When radio waves bounce off an object, they are deflected, or turned aside, by features on the object's surface. By studying the deflections, we can tell what the object looks like, even when we can't see it.

In 1978, a US probe called Pioneer Venus was put into orbit around Venus. Using its radar, it made a map of the entire planet. Radar from the Venera probes has also helped astronomers get a fuller picture of Venus's surface. Venus has no oceans, and only a few craters, so it is not like either Earth or the Moon.

Opposite: Since 1978, the US Pioneer Orbiter has studied the planet's atmosphere and mapped its surface using radar beams.

Below: Several continent-sized regions are evident on radar maps of Venus. The largest, Aphrodite Terra (lower), is about half the size of Africa. The north polar area (circle at top) remains unmapped.

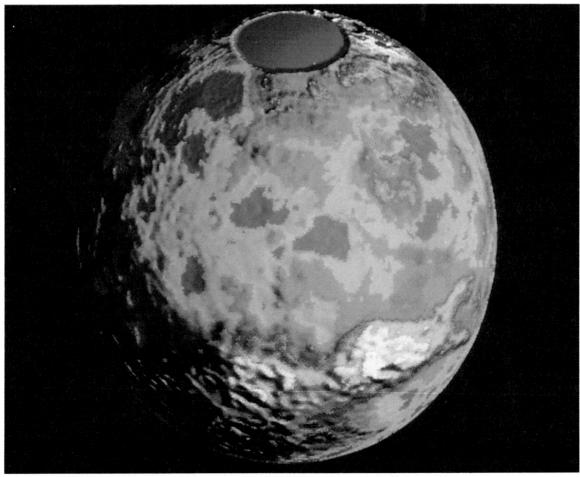

The Map of Venus

Venus is mostly flat. Earth's surface is made up of pieces called "plates" that slowly move, carrying the continents with them. Sometimes two plates come together and form mountains, like the Himalayas, or cause earthquakes, as in California. But from what we can tell so far, Venus's surface is all one single plate.

Above: Combining data from several sources, including US and Russian Venus probes, scientists have created this view of the Ishtar Terra region (yellow, near center). The lighter the color, the higher the altitude. Below: Maxwell Montes (orange), the highest mountains on Venus, tower above the flat Lakshmi Planum (purple) area.

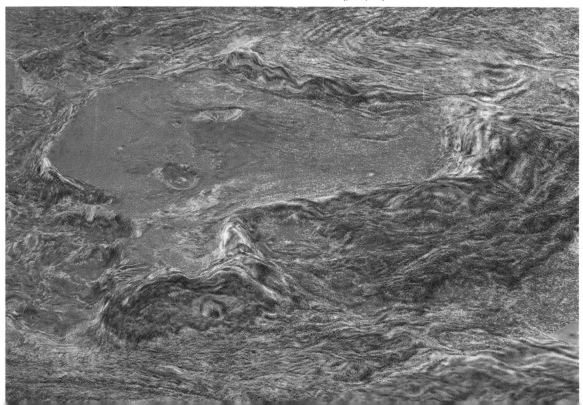

There are two areas on Venus that are higher than the rest of the surface, almost like continents on Earth. They contain mountains, some of them higher than any on Earth, and canyons, and what look like extinct volcanoes.

The larger "continent" in the north is called Ishtar Terra, after the Babylonian goddess of love. It is about the size of the United States. The smaller one, named Aphrodite Terra, after the Greek goddess of love, is near the equator. All features on Venus are given women's names, by an agreement of the International Astronomical Union (IAU). This is the group that decides on the names for everything astronomers find in space.

The US Magellan space probe starts its journey from the payload bay of the space shuttle Atlantis. Magellan is designed to provide high-quality radar images of Venus.

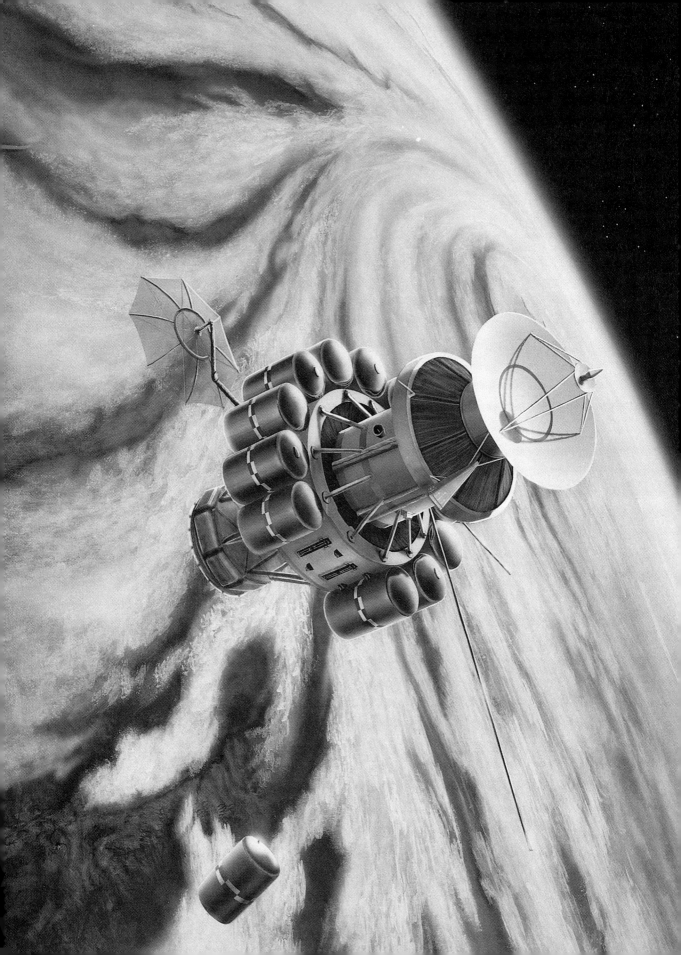

Urban Renewal, Venus Style

Venus is so close to Earth, and so nearly the same size, that it seems quite likely the two planets were similar when they first came into existence. But they developed very differently.

Venus may once have had oceans, like Earth, although we have no way of telling whether they lasted long enough for life to begin. There are still traces of water on Venus today, in the clouds in the form of water vapor.

Some people think that one day we will be able to transform other planets to make them more Earth-like. This is called terraforming. If the clouds on Venus were seeded with plant cells, they might start changing the carbon dioxide into oxygen. This would cause the planet to cool down and become livable. Perhaps some day we will try this experiment.

Below: an artist's rendering of the Ashen Light, for hundreds of years one of Venus's most fascinating mysteries.

The Ashen Light — fact or figment?

For centuries, observers looking at a crescent Venus have sometimes been able to see the dark part of its disk dimly lit with a faint rusty brown glow. No one knows what causes this. Could it be auroras or lightning on Venus, or reflected light from our own planet? Some astronomers don't believe it exists at all. If it's an optical illusion, no one can explain what it is. So for now, it remains one of Venus's most baffling mysteries.

?

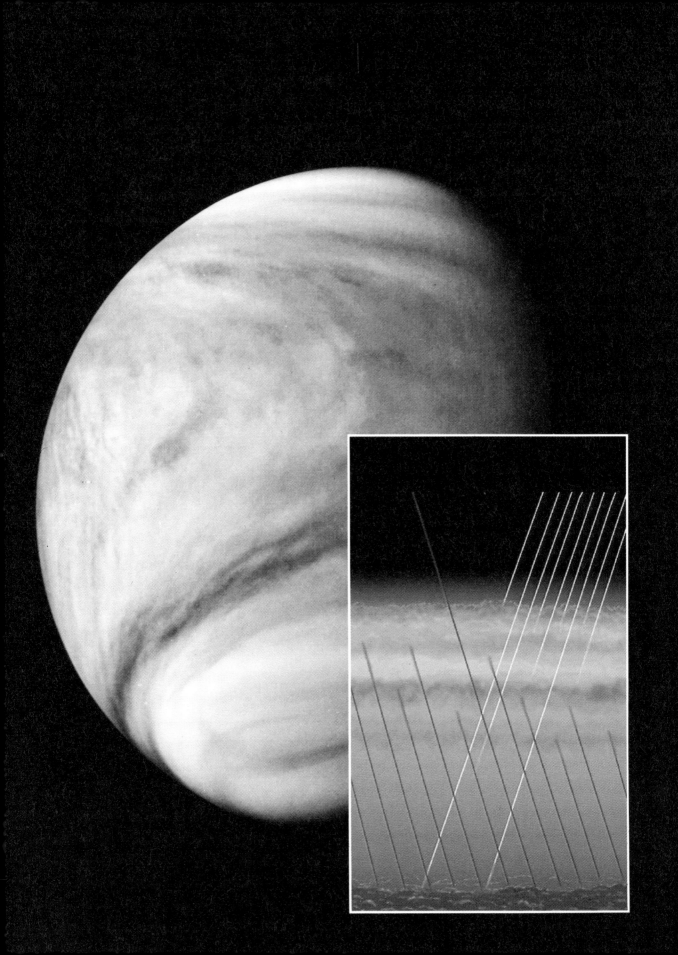

The Greenhouse Effect — What Went Wrong?

If Venus was like Earth to begin with, why did it change? Because Venus is nearer to the Sun than Earth is, it was always warmer. More of its oceans would have evaporated, putting more water vapor in the atmosphere. Water vapor helps hold more of the Sun's heat. This is called the greenhouse effect.

Venus would have gotten still warmer, producing still more water vapor. Carbon dioxide dissolved into the ocean would have begun to bubble out as the water grew steadily hotter. Carbon dioxide in the air also holds onto the Sun's heat, speeding up the process. The temperature would continue to rise until the oceans began to boil — a runaway greenhouse effect. Finally there would be no oceans left, and the temperature would become like that of the inside of a furnace.

We can't be sure that this is what happened on Venus. Whatever happened, Earth has been lucky, at least for now. But some people are afraid that our polluted air will raise the level of carbon dioxide and will cause the same thing to happen here someday.

In a greenhouse on Earth (below), glass walls admit the warming rays of sunlight but keep infrared radiation (heat) from leaving. Something similar happens in Venus's cloudy atmosphere. Opposite (inset): Sunlight (white lines) falls on Venus, but gases in the atmosphere keep heat (red lines) from escaping.

In all the unbelievably vast Universe, there is only one world that we actually live on, where the whole drama of the life we know began. That world is Earth, our home, one small planet circling one middle-sized star in a corner of a single unremarkable galaxy. Just the same, Earth is a marvelous world that we must not take for granted. After all, it has *us* on it! *Isaac Asimov*

EARTH: Our Home Base

The Birth of Earth

Nearly five billion years ago, there was a vast cloud of dust and gas that was slowly swirling. Its gravitational pull forced it closer and closer together. As it grew smaller, it whirled faster and grew hotter at the center.

Beyond the very center of the cloud, the dust and gas built up into rocks and boulders. At the very center of the cloud it got so hot that a star developed — our Sun.

Meanwhile, the rocks and boulders gradually came together with leftover gas to form the planets of our Solar system. One of the planets that formed was our Earth!

Left: Planets form in the swirling disk of gas and dust surrounding the newborn Sun.

Below: The young Earth sweeps up some of the rocky leftovers of the Solar system's birth.

91

Above: Glowing as it travels through the new atmosphere, rocky debris crashes onto Earth's hot surface.

Right: Even today, gases escape from within our planet.

Earth's Growing Pains

Earth was quite hot as it formed, and the last pieces that joined it left marks on the planet's surface. These marks are called craters. The Moon formed nearby, and you can still see the craters on it.

Water and gases were trapped in the rocks. The water and gases slowly fizzed out to form Earth's vast oceans and Earth's atmosphere.

Slowly, the heaviest parts of the Earth — metals such as iron — settled to the center and melted to form a hot metal core. Around the core, a rocky mantle of solid matter formed. The mantle is hot enough to be slightly soft. The rock in the mantle slowly moves.

Right: The Moon has changed little since it formed. Its craters are the scars of ancient collisions.

Below: A slice through Earth would reveal several layers of different material.

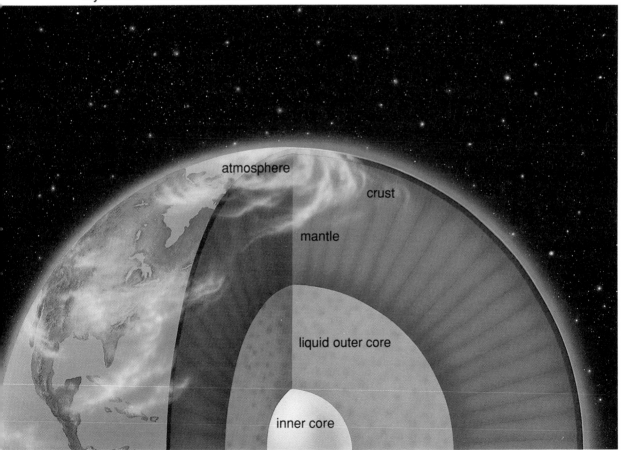

atmosphere

crust

mantle

liquid outer core

inner core

93

Our Restless Planet

The Earth's crust is not one solid shell, but is broken into many pieces called plates. These plates move slowly but steadily, so Earth's face is constantly changing.

Hundreds of millions of years ago, all of Earth's continents were in one supercontinent. We call this continent Pangaea (pronounced pan-GEE-ah). Slowly, Earth's moving plates pulled Pangaea apart into the seven continents as we know them today.

Where the plates pull apart, hot rock comes up from beneath and forms mountains in the middle of ocean floors. Sometimes the tops of the mountains are visible above the ocean. We call these mountaintops islands — like the Hawaiian Islands or the Azores.

Earth looked quite different millions of years ago. At one time, all the land areas were joined together in one giant continent scientists call Pangaea.

What a waterful world!

Earth's oceans are much larger than Earth's continents. Europe, Asia, and Africa have a combined area of 32,330,000 square miles (about 83,735,000 square km). That's 5/9 of all the land on Earth! But the Pacific Ocean, all by itself, is 64,186,300 square miles (about 166,243,000 square km) in area, so it is twice as large as Asia, Europe, and Africa put together. If you consider the other oceans, about 71% of the Earth's surface is covered with water!

If measured from their underwater bases, the mountains of the Hawaiian Islands are the tallest on Earth.

Our largest mountain range also lies under the sea. The Mid-Atlantic Ridge stretches 10,000 miles (16,000 km), cutting the Atlantic Ocean down the middle. Hot rock from deep within the Earth builds the mountains as the seafloor spreads apart.

Earth's Rumblings

Just as the plates are pulling apart in some places, they must come together in other places. This collision of plates can cause the crust to crumple.

Tens of millions of years ago, India bumped into Asia, and the crumpling of the crust created the Himalaya Mountains. The Rocky Mountains in North America were created by the collision of the Pacific and North American plates.

Sometimes, the plates rub past one another. But the plates don't slide smoothly against one another. They jerk along, under great tension. We feel these jerks as earthquakes. The boundaries of these sliding plates are marked by cracks, or faults, across the Earth's surface.

India's collision with Asia built the Himalaya Mountains into the highest place on Earth.

Mt. Everest — just a sinking sensation?

Earth's ocean is deeper than mountains are high! The highest mountain is Mt. Everest. Its peak is 29,028 ft (about 5 1/2 miles or 8.9 km) above sea level. But at a place in the Pacific called the Challenger Deep, the ocean floor is 36,161 ft (about 6.8 miles or 11 km) below sea level. If Mt. Everest could be put in the Challenger Deep, the whole mountain would sink into the ocean, and water 1.3 miles (about 2 km) deep would roll above its peak!

Above: the San Andreas Fault in California. Pressure builds as plates try to grind past each other. When the rocks give way — earthquake!

Above and right: Earthquakes can topple buildings and reshape the Earth.

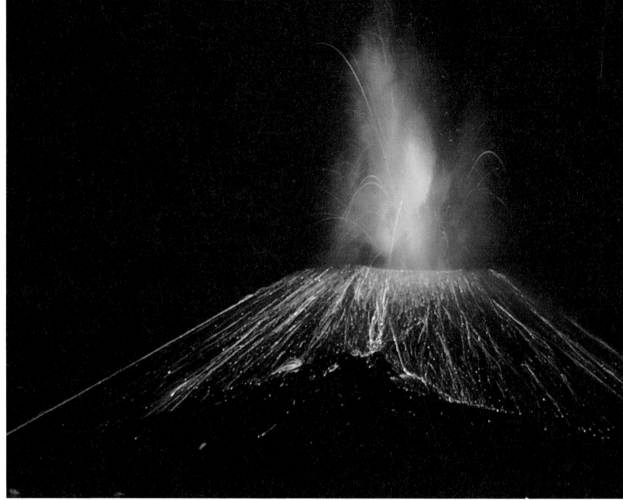

Parícutin in Mexico started as a smoking crack in a cornfield. Within eight years, it destroyed two villages and grew to over 1,300 feet (400 m).

Earth's Inner Fires

Where plates meet, one slides under the other. As one plate sinks, its rock is heated to the melting point. This melted rock makes its way upward and produces volcanoes.

In Hawaii, there is an active volcano, Kilauea (kee-lu-A-ah) Crater, where melted rock, or lava, sometimes overflows in a river of fire. There was a volcanic eruption at Mt. St. Helens in Washington State a few years ago.

Most of the ocean floor beneath the Pacific is one big plate. All around its edge, there are volcanoes and earthquakes. Because of all this activity, the edge is known as the Ring of Fire.

Violent things like earthquakes and volcanoes are Earth's way of adjusting to changing pressures at and below its surface. But these things can have terrible results for us, since they can destroy homes and kill hundreds, or even thousands, of people.

Lava, Hawaiian style. Above: a fountain of molten rock from Hawaii's Kilauea volcano. Left: fresh lava. Right: an aerial view of a lava river oozing down Kilauea's slope.

Below: Volcanoes — surface and submarine alike — form above hot spots of molten rock (lower arrows) caused by one plate riding over another. The upper arrows indicate a break in the seafloor allowing molten rock to form underwater mountains (left) and a fault line along the rim of the ocean (right).

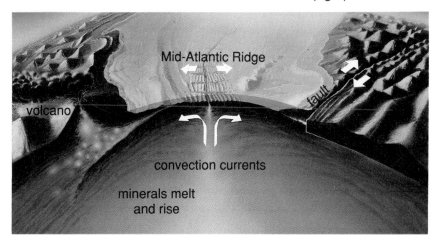

Mid-Atlantic Ridge

volcano

fault

convection currents

minerals melt and rise

The island that exploded

The greatest volcanic eruption in modern times took place in 1883 on a little Indonesian island called Krakatau. When that island — really a volcano — exploded, it set up a huge wave of water that washed over nearby shores and destroyed 163 villages. Over 36,000 people were drowned. The explosion was so loud that it could be heard 3,000 miles (4,800 km) away. Rocks were hurled 34 miles (55 km) into the air! We are lucky that volcanoes only rarely explode.

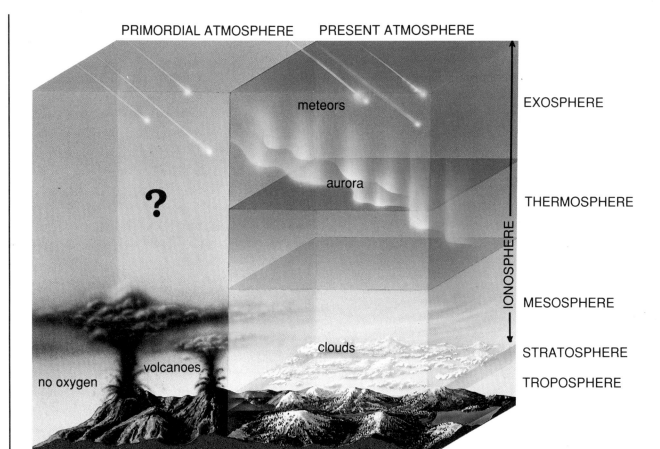

PRIMORDIAL ATMOSPHERE   PRESENT ATMOSPHERE

EXOSPHERE

meteors

aurora

THERMOSPHERE

?

IONOSPHERE

MESOSPHERE

clouds

STRATOSPHERE

no oxygen   volcanoes

TROPOSPHERE

Earth's atmosphere wasn't always as pleasant as it is now.

The Atmosphere — An "Ocean" of Air

Earth is surrounded by a vast amount of air. At first, this atmosphere was made up of nitrogen and carbon dioxide. But as simple forms of life developed, they changed the carbon dioxide to oxygen, so we can breathe it now. In fact, when people and animals exhale, or breathe out, they exhale carbon dioxide into the air.

Living things change the air. Plants use the gases we exhale to make their food — and the oxygen we need to breathe.

100

The atmosphere is unevenly heated by the Sun. Warm air rises and cold air sinks, and that sets up a movement that creates the winds. Ocean water evaporates. When it reaches the upper air, it is cooled and changed into clouds made of water droplets. The water rains down on Earth. Sometimes, the combination of rain and wind can cause violent storms like hurricanes and tornadoes.

Above and below: Thunderstorms bring lightning and strong winds — sometimes even tornadoes.

Earth's Invisible Shield

As Earth turns, the melted iron in the central core swirls. The swirling iron sets up a magnetic field that surrounds the Earth. This makes Earth a big magnet! That's why compasses work. The needle always points toward Earth's magnetic poles.

The Sun is always giving off particles with electric charges. This is called the solar wind. It could harm Earth, but it is trapped in the magnetic field, so most of the solar wind doesn't reach us. But some particles reach the air in Earth's polar regions and make the atmosphere glow. The spectacular light in the sky is called the aurora.

Particles from the distant Sun (unseen, left) pull and stretch Earth's magnetic field. Most simply flow around our magnetic field, but some particles are trapped inside it. A few particles enter the atmosphere, usually over Earth's poles.

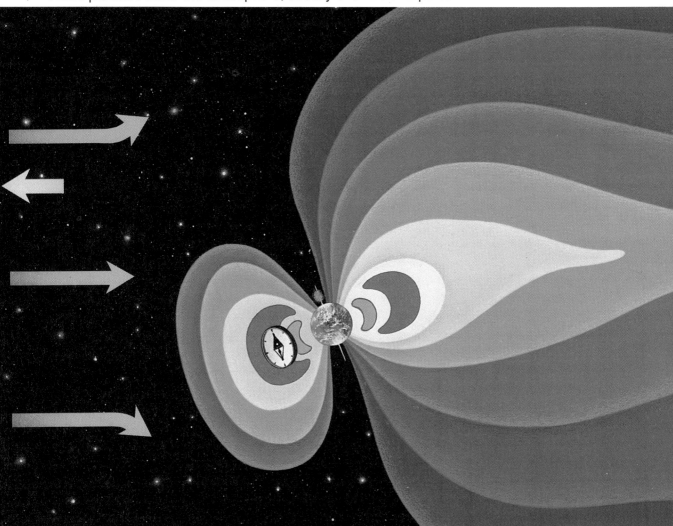

The aurora. When solar particles collide with gases in the air, the gas atoms give off light. Auroras can be as colorful as a rainbow, but green and blue-green are the most common colors.

Earth's magnetic field — time for a change?

Earth's magnetic field gets slowly stronger at times and slowly weaker at other times. Every once in a while it gets weaker and weaker until it has no strength. Then it reverses itself and starts getting stronger again. The north magnetic pole appears in the south, and the south magnetic pole appears in the north! Why does this happen? We're not sure. Right now, the field is getting weaker. By the year 4000, it might start getting stronger and reverse.

Astronauts have been able to watch Earth rise over the Moon's surface.

Exploring Earth on Alien Worlds

Nowadays, we can explore other worlds and compare them to Earth.

Like Earth, Mars has polar ice caps and a day that is about 24 hours long. But Mars is much colder than Earth. Venus has a thicker cloud layer and atmosphere than we do. A red spot on Jupiter is really a giant storm — like a hurricane that seems to go on forever. One of Jupiter's satellites, Io, has volcanic eruptions.

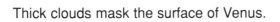

Thick clouds mask the surface of Venus.

Our Moon has no air or water
and hardly changes, so we can
use it to find out how things
were in the early days of our
Solar system.

What we learn about other worlds
can help us understand our own!

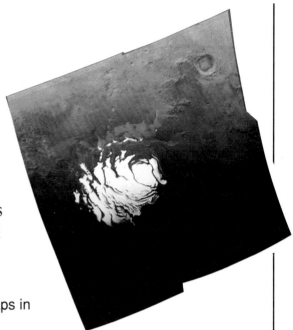

Right: Like Earth, Mars also has icy polar caps in
the far north and south.

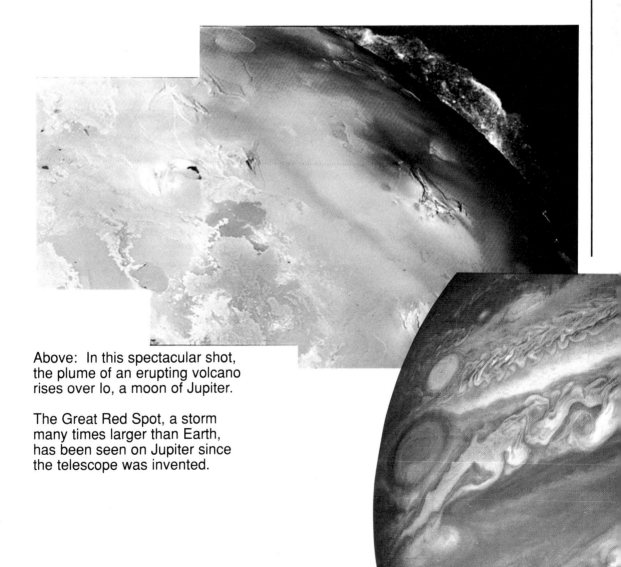

Above: In this spectacular shot,
the plume of an erupting volcano
rises over Io, a moon of Jupiter.

The Great Red Spot, a storm
many times larger than Earth,
has been seen on Jupiter since
the telescope was invented.

Spaceship Earth.

Our "Lifeboat" in Space

Other planets might help us learn about Earth. But Earth is still different from any other planet we know.

Other planets are too small to hold an atmosphere, or are too hot or too cold for water to stay liquid. Earth is the only world with a water ocean, which is needed for life to develop. So Earth is the only world on which complex life did develop.

Earth life then went on to form an oxygen atmosphere. In short, Earth is just right, the right size and the right temperature for us to live on.

There might be other worlds like Earth circling other stars, but we don't know anything about them!

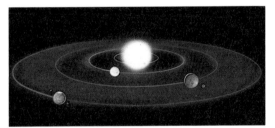

Mars is too cold, Venus too hot. Earth is just right for life.

Human beings (right) are the dominant life form on Earth. We share the planet with a great variety of living creatures, such as these Lemon Butterfly fish off the coast of Hawaii (below).

The Delicate Balance

Of course, Earth might not stay just right. Human beings do not always treat their world gently. And our numbers are increasing.

Right now, there are more than five billion of us. We need space, so we are cutting down Earth's forests and driving other forms of life to extinction. We are polluting the atmosphere and ocean, so breathing and drinking can sometimes be dangerous. We have put holes in the ozone layer, a part of our atmosphere that helps shield us from harmful radiation. Then, too, we have nuclear bombs that could make Earth's surface radioactive — and life impossible.

We must try to take better care of our precious world!

Right: air pollution from smokestacks.

Below: Water pollution hurts animals and people, too.

14 BILLION POUNDS

Amount of trash dumped annually into the world's oceans.

10

5

0

TRASH

A layer of ozone gas protects us from the Sun's harmful rays. Yet many human products are damaging its ability to help us.

Rain forests (left) are shrinking all over the world. Trees are cut down so the land may be used by people (below).

A hole zone in our ozone? Where will it lead?

Scientists warn that certain gases in air conditioners and spray cans could destroy Earth's ozone layer. Ozone is a form of oxygen, and small amounts of it exist 15 miles (24 km) above Earth's surface. It stops the Sun's damaging ultraviolet rays. Right now, the ozone layer seems to be getting thinner! In fact, there is a hole in it over Antarctica during its winter. Will it completely disappear — and what will that mean for us? Scientists aren't sure.

One day, perhaps, our cities will be easier on the environment.
Pollution will be a thing of the past.

Leaving Earth

We can explore other worlds with telescopes and rocket probes. But human beings have begun to go closer to those worlds themselves. K. E. Tsiolkovsky, a Russian scientist and rocket pioneer, said: "Earth is humanity's cradle, but you can't stay in the cradle forever."

In 1969, a human being stepped on the Moon for the first time in history. A total of 12 human beings have now walked on the Moon. We are making plans for human beings to visit Mars some day. We are hoping to have permanent space stations where human beings can work. Perhaps we will one day build whole towns in space where thousands of people can live.

Cities in space? Why not! We are just beginning to explore the possibilities of living and working in space.

It's hard to imagine a time when your school bus will be a rocket ship, but it might happen someday!

New Earths

Some day, it might be possible for human beings to make new homes on other worlds. We may build domed cities on the Moon and Mars. Or it might be better to burrow underneath the ground. It might even be possible to bring water and oxygen to Mars and make a new Earth of it. We might be able to take some of the carbon dioxide away from Venus and turn the rest into oxygen. That would cool Venus, which is now just too hot for us.

Making other planets like Earth, or terraforming them, is something we cannot do now. But we will surely have greater powers in a century or two. Then, too, the day will come when we can visit other stars. We might find planets so much like Earth that they will not need terraforming!

But for now, Earth's future is <u>our</u> future. Let's take good care of both!

As we move to the other planets in our Solar system, we might try to change their climates for the better. Perhaps the Sun will one day peek through the thick clouds of Venus to shine on a beach full of vacationers.

Thousands of years ago, people watched the sky and noticed that certain bright stars shifted position from night to night. The Greeks called them "wandering stars." Naturally, they called them that in the Greek language. Those words have come down to us to mean "planet."

One of these planets has a reddish color, almost the color of blood. It was therefore named after the god of war, Mars, since so much blood is spilled in war. In this chapter, we'll tell you about the planet Mars and what we have learned about it recently.

Isaac Asimov

MARS:
Our
Mysterious
Neighbor

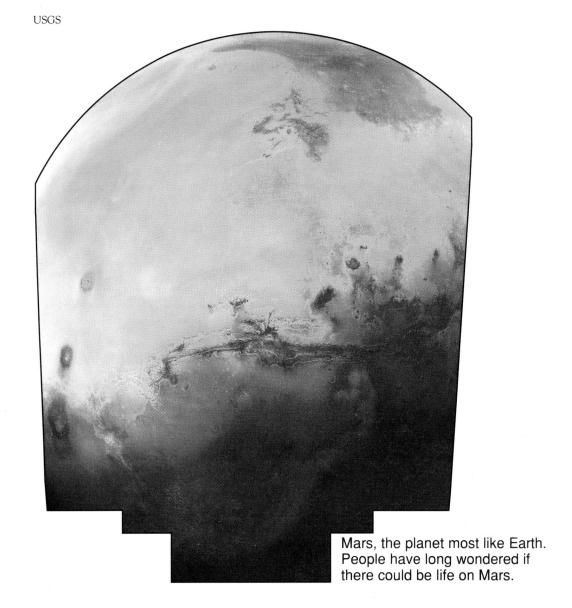

Mars, the planet most like Earth. People have long wondered if there could be life on Mars.

The Mystery of Mars

Let's leave Earth, heading away from the Sun. Mars is the first planet we come to. What do we know about our neighbor Mars? We know quite a bit, but Mars is a mysterious planet, too. We know that it is smaller than Earth. It is only half as wide as Earth, and it has only one-tenth Earth's mass. Still, Mars turns, or rotates, once every 24 1/2 hours. Its axis is tipped so that it has seasons like Earth's. Mars is colder, though, because it is farther from the Sun. It has ice caps at the poles. Of all the planets in our Solar system, it is most like Earth, so people naturally wondered if there were living creatures on Mars. If so, what were they like? That was the big mystery.

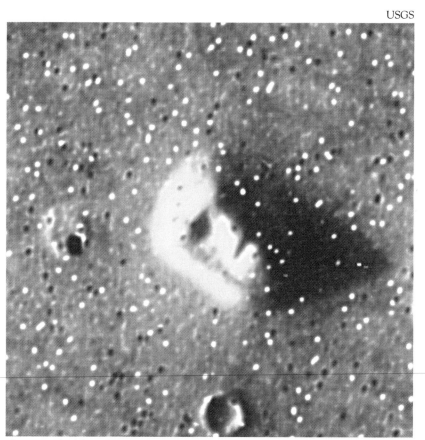

A remarkable photo of a detail on the surface of
Mars. Doesn't the object in the center look like a face?

Sunrise on Mars: a color-enhanced shot of the Martian landscape,
with a striking view of the Viking lander in the foreground.

A Desert World

We know that living creatures would have a hard time on Mars. Early astronomers could tell that it had only a thin atmosphere and that it must have very little water on it. Its surface might be one large desert. In 1877, however, narrow, dark markings were seen on Mars. These were studied by an American astronomer, Percival Lowell. He thought they were canals, dug by intelligent Martians to bring water from the ice caps at the poles to the desert areas in the rest of Mars. Lowell wrote several books on the subject, and for a while many people were sure there was intelligent life on Mars.

Lowell Observatory

Percival Lowell in a 1905 photograph. Here, he looks at Venus by daylight through a telescope that has been in continuous use since 1897.

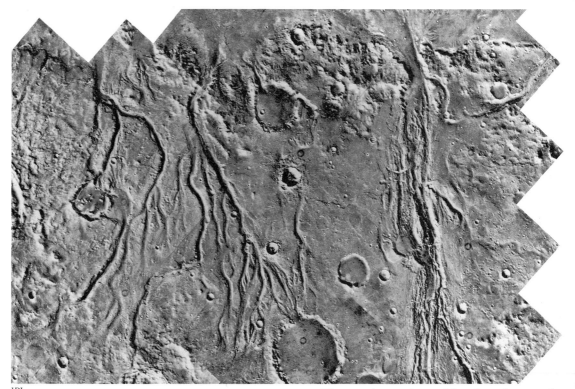

JPL

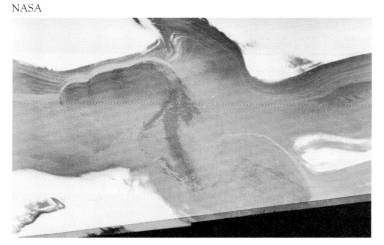

NASA

These channels on Mars' surface may have been carved by running water in Mars' distant past. These are not the same as the "canals" seen by Lowell. Astronomers now think the canals were an optical illusion.

Here is summer at Mars' North Pole. Clouds over the polar cap have cleared to reveal water ice, as well as the layered terrain beneath it.

Calling all Martians!

People were once so sure that Mars had intelligent beings on it that ways were thought up of sending them messages. One scientist suggested that huge triangles and squares be dug in Siberia, filled with oil, and set on fire at night. The Martians would see these through their telescopes, and then they might arrange something for us to see in return. Even as late as 1938, the actor Orson Welles presented a radio play in which Martians were said to be invading New Jersey. He frightened hundreds of people who got into their cars and drove away to escape those Martians — who really didn't exist.

Moon-like Mars?

For years and years, people thought about the chances of life on Mars. Finally, when scientists learned how to send rockets to Mars, it seemed we would get some answers. In 1964, a Mars probe, Mariner 4, was sent out to Mars. In July, 1965, this probe passed within 6,000 miles (9,600 km) of the planet, and took 19 close-up photographs which it beamed back to Earth. These photographs showed craters on Mars like those on the Moon. Mars' atmosphere turned out to be only 1/100 as thick as Earth's, and there was no sign of any canals. Mars seemed to be a dead world.

NASA

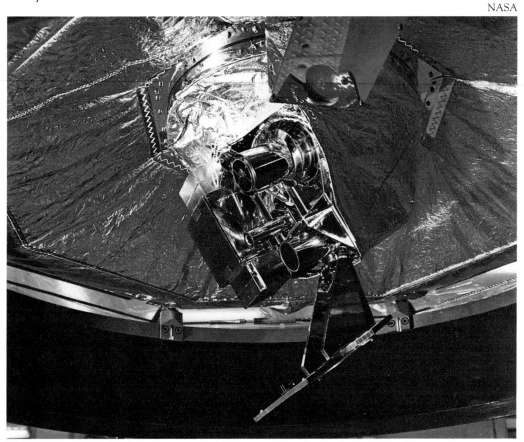

The Mariner 4 television camera. The camera took pictures as it passed Mars, stored them on tape, and beamed them back to Earth. Each picture took about eight hours to play back, or reconstruct, from the radio transmission. The whole transmission lasted over seven days!

Left: The moon-like southern regions of Mars. After years of thinking about the possibility of life on Mars, scientists know it's not likely. Many people were relieved, but others were disappointed. How do you feel about it? Would you have liked to meet Martians?   JPL

Look Again!

In 1971, another Mars probe, Mariner 9, reached Mars. It went into orbit about Mars and took many photographs. It mapped almost the entire planet. There were definitely no canals. The photos showed that the straight, dark lines were just illusions. The photos also showed many craters on Mars, but also flatter areas with extinct volcanoes. One of these, named Olympus Mons, was far larger than any volcano on Earth. The pictures also showed a huge canyon, named Valles Marineris, that was far larger than our own Grand Canyon. Mars' surface proved to be much more interesting than that of the Moon. But it still seemed a dead world.

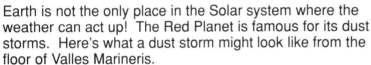

JPL

Earth is not the only place in the Solar system where the weather can act up! The Red Planet is famous for its dust storms. Here's what a dust storm might look like from the floor of Valles Marineris.

© John Foster 1988

NASA

Ten Viking 1 pictures make up this image of a portion of western Valles Marineris. The channel-like formations were probably dug out by the wind and by the downhill flow of debris during ice thaws.

Olympus Mons, Mars' extinct volcano: This is the largest known volcano in the Solar system. This is a false-color photo taken by a Viking probe.

Mars — fooling the pros

Why did Percival Lowell see canals on Mars when there weren't any? He was a good astronomer with excellent telescopes. He worked on high ground in Arizona where the air was very clear. It's possible that he could just barely make out little dark patches on Mars. His eyes, not knowing what to make of them, saw them as straight lines. People have experimented with schoolchildren looking at distant circles with little dark patches. The children reported they saw straight lines. This is called an optical illusion. Maybe that's what fooled Lowell.

A New Look at Mars

In 1976, two new Mars probes arrived, Viking 1 and Viking 2. These were not there just to go into orbit about the planet. They were actually going to put landers on the Martian surface. They did this successfully. And while passing through the atmosphere, they analyzed it. The Martian atmosphere is about 95 percent carbon dioxide, and most of the rest is nitrogen and argon. This means that the Martian atmosphere has almost no oxygen in it. What's more the Martian surface is as cold as Antarctica or colder. So any water on Mars must be frozen.

More strange markings

The Mars probes have discovered strange markings on Mars. These markings look like dry river channels that form crookedly across the surface as real rivers would. Smaller channels run into larger ones just as smaller rivers run into larger ones on Earth. It seems almost certain that at one time in the past, Mars may have had liquid water forming rivers and, perhaps, lakes. In that case, what happened to the water? Is it now all frozen in the soil? And if Mars once had water and rivers, was the atmosphere thicker, then, and was there life on Mars, then? So far, we just don't know.

In 1976, Mars was photographed by Viking 1 from 348,000 miles (557,000 km) above the planet. Olympus Mons is visible near the upper left edge of the planet. Just to its right are the three volcanoes of the Tharsis ridge.

NASA

The Viking test lander: The front footpad of this model rests on a rock, as the actual lander did on Mars. As a result, cameras in the lander showed the Martian horizon to be sloped. In fact, it is nearly perfectly level.

© John Waite 1987

At 86,592 feet (26,400   m), Olympus Mons is easily taller than any of Earth's peaks. The back row shows the Martian peaks. Center row, left to right, shows Earth's Mt. Everest (29,028 ft / 8,850 m), Mt. Rainier (14,410 ft / 4,393 m), and Mont Blanc (15,771 ft / 4,808 m). Front row shows Mt. Fuji (12,388 ft / 3,777 m) and Mt. St. Helens (9,677 ft / 2,950 m).

The Search for Life

The Viking probes took photographs of Mars' surface. But they also did more, for they carried equipment that could test the Martian soil. If the soil contained microscopic forms of life, the tests would show chemical changes. The probes scooped up soil and tested it in three different ways to see if such changes took place. There were changes, but it wasn't certain they were the result of life. However, nothing was detected in the soil that contained carbon, which is essential to our kind of life. Yes, the surface of Mars may be more interesting than that of our Moon. But it may still be that Mars is a dead world.

The surface of Mars looks like a rocky desert on Earth. The probes scooped up some of the Martian soil to test for life. None of our tests showed any signs of life.

NASA

The Martian horizon as photographed by the Viking lander. The lower center of this beautiful shot shows trenches left by the lander's sampling tools on the surface of Mars.

NASA

Another view of Mars from the lander. This is a colored shot of an area similar to that shown in black and white on page 126.

The Moons of Mars

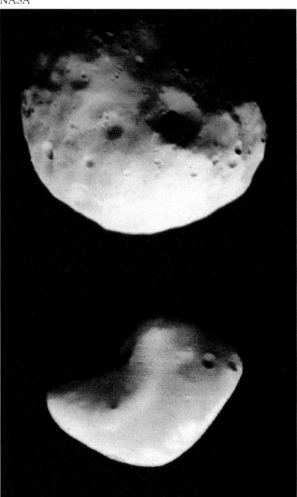

Mars has two small satellites, or moons, called Phobos and Deimos. They are not large globes like our own Moon, but they may be captured satellites that once passed Mars and were drawn into orbit by Mars' gravitational field. From Earth, they look like two dim dots of light, but the probes showed them more clearly. They are shaped like potatoes and are covered with craters. Phobos is 17 miles (27 km) across at its longest. Deimos is only 10 miles (16 km) across. Because of their small size and their closeness to Mars, these little satellites were not discovered till 1877. This was long after the more distant but larger satellites of Jupiter and Saturn were discovered.

Martian satellites. Top: Phobos. Bottom: Deimos. Phobos orbits Mars in about seven hours and 40 minutes. Deimos orbits in about 30 hours.

If at first you don't succeed...

The Martian satellites were discovered by an American astronomer named Asaph Hall. Night after night in 1877, he looked through his telescope at the space near Mars and could find nothing. Finally, he made up his mind that it was no use. He said to his wife, whose maiden name was Angelina Stickney, that he was giving up. His wife said, "Try it one more night." He did, and discovered the satellites. Now the largest crater on the satellite Phobos is named "Stickney" in honor of the woman who urged Hall not to give up.

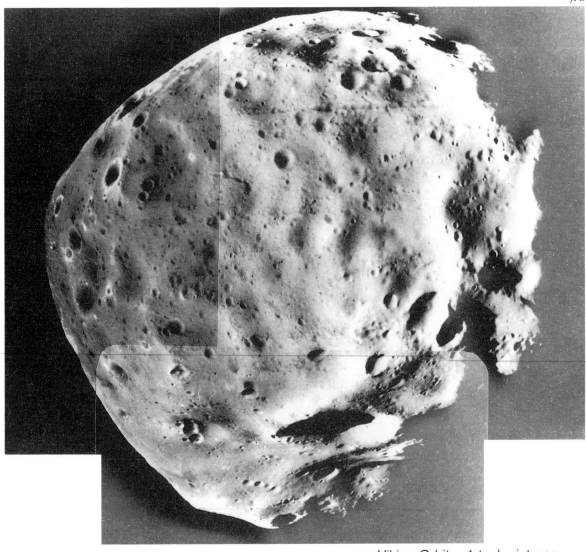

© Michael Carroll 1987

Viking Orbiter 1 took pictures that were combined to create this image of Phobos. The craters you see were probably caused by the impact of space debris.

The 1989 Soviet (now referred to as Russian) Phobos mission. One of its goals is to drop landers on Phobos to map its surface and subsurface and study its composition.

A Handful of Mars

Mars is much farther than the Moon and much harder to reach, but scientists are planning further probes. Both the Russian Federation and the US are planning to send probes to Mars and Phobos—including a possible joint Russian/US mission that will land and unload an automatic car like one used on the Moon. It could travel for miles across the Martian surface, studying the surface as it goes. Other probes might dig down and test the soil well beneath the surface. Even more exciting are probes that might collect samples of soil and then send them back to Earth. Such soil could be tested in great detail here on our own planet.

Phobos—a moon in a hurry!

*Phobos is only 5,810 miles (9,296 km) from Mars' center. Compare this with the Moon, which is over 238,000 miles (380,800 km) from Earth's center. The closer a satellite is to a planet, the faster that satellite moves. It takes the Moon almost four weeks to go around the Earth. Phobos travels around Mars in 7.65 **hours**! It travels about Mars faster than Mars turns on its axis! Phobos overtakes Mars, so if you were standing on Mars' surface, you would see Phobos rise in the west, hurry across the sky, and set in the east.*

One design of a possible Mars mission vehicle. Note the streamlined shape. This would help the probe maneuver in Mars' atmosphere to slow it down during its approach.

© Kurt Burmann 1986

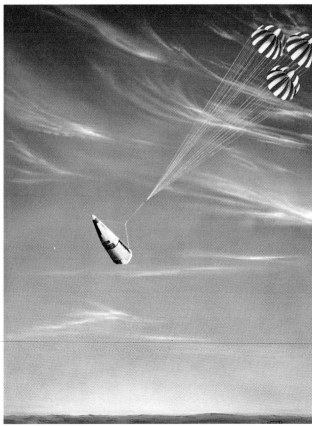

Parachutes would allow this probe
to float gently to the surface of
Mars.

An artist imagines a joint US/Russian mission with two rovers
scurrying across the dusty surface of Mars.

A joint US/Russian piloted mission to Mars might be possible. The astronauts and cosmonauts could be gone from Earth for two years, so it would be helpful if the crew spoke both English and Russian!

Voyage to the Red Planet

Think of how much we'd still be wondering about Mars if not for fancy probes like Mariner and Viking. But no matter how fancy these probes might be, we could do so much more if spaceships carried astronauts to Mars. This would not be an easy task, for it might take nearly two years to go and return. Some people think it might be too big a job for any one nation.

Perhaps the United States and the Russian Federation, working together, could send a combined expedition to Mars. They could explore our mysterious neighbor, and study its craters, canyons, volcanoes, ice caps, and whatever else they find. What we learn may help us better understand our own planet, Earth.

Fog in a Martian canyon. In the background are
ice-covered mountains. Nothing is liquid on Mars
anymore, though there may once have been water
in a liquid form.

A beautiful watchtower formation at Kasei Vallis, Mars. This might
make a two-year trip to Mars worthwhile to someone who really
<u>loves</u> to travel. How about you?

Colonies on Mars

What else might we do if we were able to send people to Mars? We can imagine colonies on the Moon, since the Moon is only three days' rocket-time away from Earth. Mars is much farther away, but in some ways it is an easier world to live on. It has a gravitational pull that is 2/5 that of Earth, while the Moon's is only 1/6 that of Earth. Mars has a thin atmosphere that can protect people from meteors and radiation a bit, while the Moon has none. Mars has some water, while the Moon has none. We can imagine cities built underground on Mars, or perhaps domed cities on the surface. And if we do count the Moon, human beings will then be living on three different worlds.

A mission carrying people flies past Phobos and makes its final approach to the Red Planet. Crew members work on a communication satellite that will let them tell Earth's residents how they like what they find.

© Paul DiMare 1985

Mars from Phobos. To explorers stationed on Phobos,
Mars would loom large and red.

A futuristic colony on Mars. A total artificial environment — one inside
buildings, space suits, and vehicles — would make the Martian
atmosphere fit for humans. Landing at the colony would be easy
enough, and the rocket launch site would allow people to leave as well.

Exploring Mars

What would space explorers do on Mars? Once settlements are established on Mars, exploring parties can be sent out. Imagine some of them, in special cars, driving along the bottom of a canyon that stretches for 3,000 miles (4,800 km). Imagine a party climbing a giant volcano and studying the inside of the crater. Think of explorers making their way across the Martian ice caps at its poles. We know the ice caps contain frozen carbon dioxide, as well as frozen water. But we could learn even more about Mars from the ice caps. We might find interesting minerals, or even matter that will help us understand what Mars was like millions of years ago.

© Michael Carroll 1987

The South Pole of Mars has something major in common with Earth's South Pole — ice!

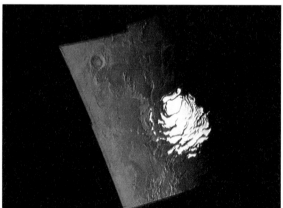

USGS

Glaciers of ice crawl across the Martian surface. Millions of years ago, creeping glaciers formed the hills and valleys of Earth with the same slow, relentless movement.

When human beings land on Mars, they can explore the insides of inactive volcanoes like this one — the Hecates Tholus Lava Tube.

The moons of Mars — a clue to life on Earth?

Phobos and Deimos don't look like Mars. Mars has a light reddish surface, but Phobos and Deimos have dark surfaces. That is probably because the satellites were once asteroids. There are certain dark meteorites that occasionally land on Earth. They contain small amounts of water and carbon-containing compounds, somewhat resembling those found in living things. Maybe it would be more interesting to study the surface of the satellites than of Mars. Wouldn't this help us decide how life originated on Earth? We'll only find out if we go there.

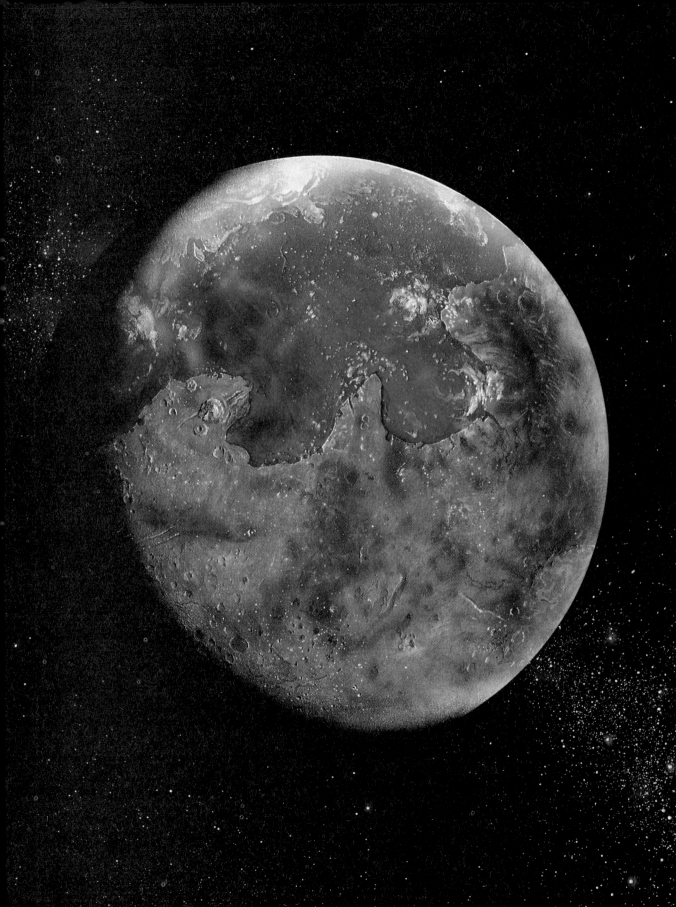

The Red and Blue Planet?

Many other, even more exciting things might be possible on Mars. The early settlers on Mars might be able to do things to make the planet more like Earth. This is called terraforming. Perhaps large supplies of water can be brought in from the asteroids. If the right gases are added to the atmosphere, Mars would trap more sunlight and grow warmer. The water won't freeze, in that case, but will form an ocean. Enough oxygen might be added to make the air breathable. Many plants and animals could be brought to Mars.

It may take many, many years, but perhaps Mars can someday become a little Earth.

On a terraformed Mars humans would not have to depend on artificial devices to breathe, keep warm or cool, or supply themselves with water. The new climate would sustain human life "naturally."

© Julian Baum 1988

Left: Here's a hot idea for the future: If we altered the climate and atmosphere of Mars by terraforming, we could melt the northern ice cap to create a large sea.　　© Michael Carroll 1985

Fact Files

Fact File: Our Solar System

The Milky Way and Our Solar System: Home, Sweet Home!

For us in the Solar system, it all began in roughly the same remote corner of the Milky Way Galaxy in which we live today. Nearly five billion years ago, our Sun took shape out of a swirling cloud of gas and dust called a nebula. A few "short" million years later, the planets evolved out of the swirling Solar nebula. Today, the Solar system seems a pretty comfortable place.

A view from our perch on the inner edge of the Orion arm of the Milky Way. The swirling galactic center glows thousands of light-years away (upper two pictures). A closer look into the Solar system (lower left) reveals the Sun, planets, and major moons according to their relative sizes.

The Sun from Start to Finish

Here is the life of our Sun from start to finish — from the first contractions of gas and dust into a Solar nebula nearly five billion years ago, to what we expect will be its final form, that of a cold black dwarf, tens of billions of years later. The form of the Sun as we know it — what astronomers call its "main sequence" — actually lasts for only about 10 billion years. This 10-billion-year period begins when nuclear fusion takes place in the Sun, and it ends when it becomes a red giant — about six billion years from now. You can see where these stages begin and end in the chart below. Keep in mind that the ages of the Sun are in millions of years, so 4,700 million years — the present age of the Sun — actually equals 4.7 <u>billion</u> years.

Age (millions of years)	What Happened
0	First contraction of matter from nebula into early Sun, or protostar. Early planets, or protoplanets, beginning to form within swirling rings of Solar nebula disk.
1	Hot core of protostar forms from contraction.
70	Protostar contraction ends. Nuclear fusion of hydrogen at core begins. With the "blowing away" of leftover nebular matter, the Solar system comes into its own, and the Sun fully becomes a "main sequence" star.
4,700	The Sun today.
7,000	Hydrogen at Sun's core begins to run out.
10,000	The burning of hydrogen moves outwards to a shell around helium core. As a result, Sun will burn more brightly; Earth's temperatures will begin to rise, very slowly.
10,600	Sun's life as a "main sequence" star comes to an end. First red-giant stage. Helium core ignites. Outer area of star forced outward; Earth's temperatures will be at boiling point.
10,650	Final red-giant stage begins. Earth a charred planet.
11,000	Final red-giant stage reaches maximum state. Helium fusion moves to shell around core. Dying star gives off gas and dust as a "planetary" nebula. White dwarf forms in 75,000 years.
?	White dwarf cools into a black dwarf, taking tens of billions of years.

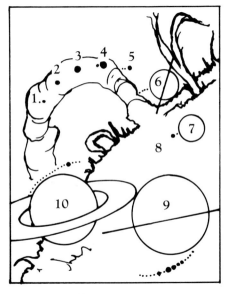

Left: a guide to the Solar system on the opposite page.

KEY	
1 — Pluto	6 — Uranus
2 — Mercury	7 — Neptune
3 — Venus	8 — Sun
4 — Earth	9 — Jupiter
5 — Mars	10 — Saturn

Fact File: Mercury

Mercury, the closest planet to the Sun, is the eighth largest known planet in our Solar system (Earth is fifth). Only Pluto is smaller. Because Mercury doesn't have an atmosphere, it has no real "weather" as we know it on Earth — only incredibly hot days, and nights just as incredibly cold. Like Venus, Mercury has no moons.

Because Mercury is so hard to see, not much was known about it until the 1960s and 1970s. Since the planet only appeared as a tiny speck that went through phases like the Moon, no one really knew what Mercury's surface was like. But thanks to Mariner 10 and other efforts by scientists to learn more about this planet, we now understand many things about Mercury that were once mysteries. But there's still a lot we would like to know about the "quick planet."

Even if human beings could visit Mercury one day in the future, not many would want to live there. By studying Mercury, however, we can learn a lot about the history of our Solar system — including the part of it where we <u>do</u> live, Earth.

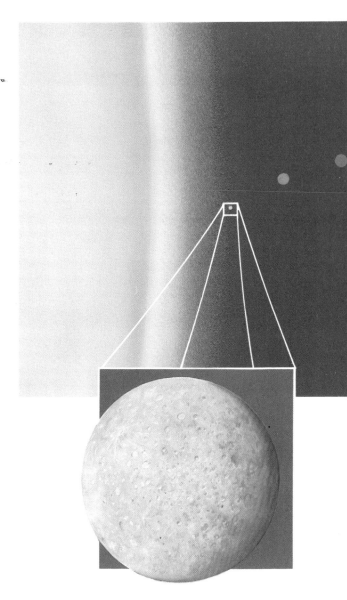

Mercury: How It Measures Up to Earth

Planet	Diameter	Rotation Period
Mercury	3,030 miles (4,875 km)	58.6 days*
Earth	7,926 miles (12,753 km)	23 hours, 56 minutes

The Sun and Its Family of Planets

Above: The Sun and its Solar system family, left to right: Mercury, Venus, Earth, Mars, Jupiter, Saturn, Uranus, Neptune, Pluto. Left: Here is a close-up of Mercury. Thanks to Mariner 10, we have pictures showing that Mercury's surface is even more heavily cratered than our Moon's.

Period of Orbit Around Sun (length of year)	Moons	Surface Gravity	Distance from Sun (nearest-farthest)	Least Time It Takes for Light to Travel to Earth
88.0 days	0	0.38**	28.5-43.3 million miles (45.9-69.7 million km)	4.4 minutes
365.25 days (one year)	1	1.00**	92-95 million miles (147-152 million km)	

* Mercury rotates, or spins on its axis, once every 58.6 days. It rotates three times for every two trips it makes around the Sun. Because Mercury rotates so slowly, the Sun stays up in Mercury's sky far longer than in Earth's sky. So from Mercury's surface, a solar "day" (sunrise to sunrise) lasts 176 days.
** Multiply your weight by this number to find out how much you would weigh on this planet.

Fact File: Venus

Venus is the sixth largest known planet in our Solar System. The second closest planet to the Sun, Venus never gets very far away from the sun in our sky. That is why Venus can only be seen just before the Sun rises in the morning or just after it sets at night. Throughout human history, Venus has been known as the Morning Star during its appearance before dawn, and the Evening Star in its appearance after dusk.

Although tiny Mercury is nearer the Sun than Venus is, it is too small and too close to the Sun to be easily spotted from Earth. Venus, on the other hand, is not only clearly visible from Earth, but it is the brightest of all the planets and stars in the sky. Only the Sun and Earth's Moon are brighter. In fact, there have been reports of Venus's "shining" brightly enough on a moonless night to cast shadows on Earth!

We know much more about Venus today than we did only a few decades ago. Since the 1960s, Russian and US probes have been studying Venus, its atmosphere, and its thick layer of clouds. It is these clouds that obscure Venus's surface, give the planet its bright appearance, and hold in the intense heat of the Sun. Thanks to the probes, Venus is no longer thought of as Earth's mysterious "twin." Yet it remains one of the most beautiful and intriguing objects to grace our sky.

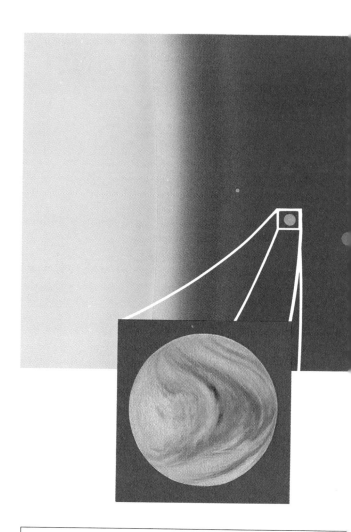

Venus: How It Measures Up to Earth

Planet	Diameter	Rotation Period
Venus	7,521 miles (12,101 km)	243 days*
Earth	7,926 miles (12,753 km)	23 hours, 56 minutes

The Sun and Its Family of Planets

Above: the Sun and its Solar system family, left to right: Mercury, Venus, Earth, Mars, Jupiter, Saturn, Uranus, Neptune, and Pluto.
Left: Here is a close-up of Venus. Thanks to the probes sent to explore Venus, we know more about the intensely hostile conditions lurking beneath — and within — the cloud cover of this lovely planet.

Period of Orbit Around Sun (length of year)	Known Moons	Surface Gravity	Distance from Sun (nearest-farthest)	Least Time It Takes for Light to Travel to Earth
24 days, 14 hours	None	0.88**	66.8-67.7 million miles (107.4-108.9 million km)	2 minutes, 6 seconds
365 days, 6 hours	1	1.00**	91.4-94.5 million miles (147-152 million km)	—

* Venus rotates, or spins on its axis, once every 243 days. But its retrograde (opposite-direction) rotation and the time it takes to orbit the Sun make a Venusian "day" — sunrise to sunrise — 117 Earth days long.
** Multiply your weight by this number to find out how much you would weigh on this planet.

Fact File: Earth

Earth is the fifth largest known planet in our Solar system, and the third closest to the Sun. It is the largest of the inner planets — just over 7,926 miles (12,756 km) wide. This means that our planet is about 5% bigger than Venus, almost twice the diameter of Mars, and more than 2 1/2 times the diameter of Mercury.

It is also the heaviest inner planet of our Solar system. Weighing in at about 6.59 sextillion (659 followed by 19 zeroes, or 6,590,000,000,000,000,000,000) tons, Earth is about 23% heavier than Venus, almost 9 1/2 times heavier than Mars, and more than 18 times the mass of Mercury.

But Earth is still only a speck compared with even an average star like our Sun. The Sun is more than 108 times the diameter of Earth. And it is almost 333,000 times as heavy!

Our planet might not be that big, but it is very important! After all, it's where we live. Human beings can — and must — learn to live together in peace, not only on Earth but wherever they might go as they explore the Universe!

Above: The Sun and its Solar system family, left to right: Mercury, Venus, Earth, Mars, Jupiter, Saturn, Uranus, Neptune, Pluto.

Earth's Moon		
Diameter	Distance from Earth's Center	Percentage of Earth's Diameter
2,160 miles (3,475 km)	242,820 miles (390,940 km)	27.25%

The Sun and Its Family of Planets

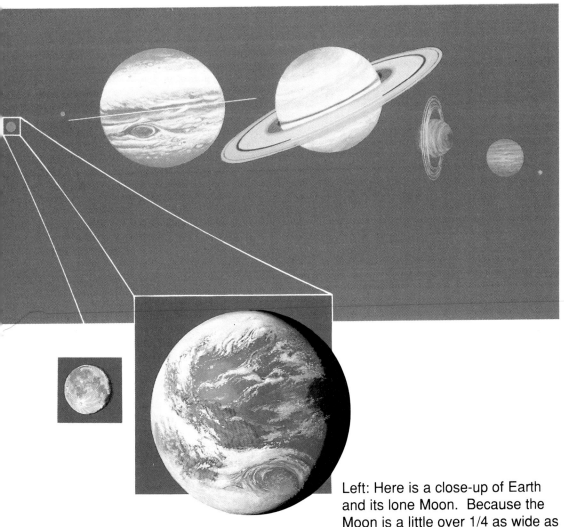

Left: Here is a close-up of Earth and its lone Moon. Because the Moon is a little over 1/4 as wide as Earth, we might think of the two as a double planet.

Compared With What We Think Is Big on Earth, Earth Is . . .	But Earth Is Also . . .
• **so wide** that if you could drill a giant hole through it and stuff the hole with clones of the world's tallest building, you could stuff 28,783 Sears Towers into the hole and still not have anything sticking out at either end! (The Sears Tower in Chicago is the world's tallest building at 1,454 feet — 443.18 m — high.) • **so big around** that even if you could drive around the world at 55 miles (88.5 km) an hour without stopping, it would still take you about 453 hours before you got back to where you started. That's almost 19 days of nonstop driving!	• **so tiny** compared to the Sun that you could stuff more than a million Earths in the space the Sun takes up! • **so far away from Mars** that it would take us about a year to get there, and another year to come back! • **our planet.** As any astronomer who has studied the Universe — or any astronaut who has seen Earth from space — can tell you, our little planet is just a speck in space. But that little speck is where we live — and the place from which we see and learn about the Universe!

Fact File: Mars

Mars is the seventh largest planet (Earth is fifth), the fourth closest to the Sun, and the first planet beyond Earth's orbit. It is also, therefore, the last of the "inner" group of planets, all of which are within the asteroid belt. Beyond the asteroids is the "outer" group that begins with Jupiter. With an axial tilt similar to Earth's and a day that is virtually the same length as ours, Mars has the same type of seasons as Earth. Of course, Mars is much farther from the Sun than Earth is, so Mars has a longer "year" than we do. This means its seasons are much longer, and its temperatures much colder, than Earth's.

Right: Here is a close-up of Mars and its two tiny but well-known satellites, Phobos (top) and Deimos (bottom).

The Moons of Mars		
Name	Diameter	Distance From Mars' Center
Phobos	13-18 miles (20-28 km)	5,827 miles (9,378 km)
Deimos	6-10 miles (10-16 km)	14,577 miles (23,459 km)

Planet	Diameter
Mars	3,973 miles (6,786 km)
Earth	7,927 miles (12,756 km)

The Sun and Its Family of Planets

The Sun and its Solar system family, left to right, above: Mercury, Venus, Earth, Mars, Jupiter, Saturn, Uranus, Neptune, Pluto.

Mars: How It Measures Up to Earth

Rotation Period (length of day)	Period of Orbit Around Sun (length of year)	Moons	Surface Gravity	Distance from Sun (nearest-farthest)	Least Time It Takes for Light to Travel to Earth
24 hours, 37 minutes	687 days (1.88 years)	2	0.38*	129-156 million miles (207-249 million km)	3.1 minutes
23 hours, 56 minutes	365.25 days (one year)	1	1.00*	92-95 million miles (147-152 million km)	—

* Multiply your weight by this number to find out how much you would weigh on this planet.

Glossary

Aphrodite Terra: one of the two "continents" on Venus, named for Aphrodite, the ancient Greek goddess of love. (See also *Ishtar Terra*.)

asteroids: very small planets and even smaller objects made of rock or metal. There are thousands of them in our Solar system, and they mainly orbit the Sun in large numbers between Mars and Jupiter. But some show up elsewhere in the Solar system—some as meteoroids and some possibly as "captured" moons of planets such as Mars.

astronomer: a person involved in the scientific study of the Universe and its various bodies.

atmosphere: the gases that surround a planet, star, or moon.

aurora: light of the North and South Poles caused by the collision of the solar wind with our outer atmosphere.

axis: the imaginary line through the center of a planet around which the planet rotates. The axis of Mars is tipped so that its seasons change as the planet orbits the Sun.

billion: in North America—and in this book—the number represented by 1 followed by nine zeroes: 1,000,000,000. In some places, such as the United Kingdom (Britain), this number is called a "a thousand million."

black hole: a massive object—usually a collapsed star—so tightly packed that not even light can escape the force of its gravity.

canal: a river or waterway made by people to move water from one place to another. It was once thought that the narrow dark markings on Mars were canals built by Martians to move water from the ice caps to the desert areas.

carbon dioxide: a gas (chemical formula CO_2) necessary for plant life. It is a colorless, heavy gas. Carbon dioxide is what gives soda its fizz, and when humans and other animals breathe, they exhale carbon dioxide.

colonies: human settlements. Many people have wondered if it might be possible to one day set up colonies on other planets or space stations or on spaceships (starships).

comet: an object made of ice, rock and gas; it has a vapor tail that may be seen when the comet's orbit is close to the Sun.

continents: large land bodies surrounded by water on Earth's surface.

Copernicus, Nicolaus: a Polish astronomer who was the first to argue that the Sun, not Earth, was the center of our Solar system and that the planets revolved around the Sun.

core: the central part of Earth. It is believed to consist of mainly iron and nickel.

craters: holes or pits on planets and moons created by volcanic explosions or the impact of meteorites.

crust: the outermost solid layer of the Earth. It includes the surface of Earth.

deeps: canyon-like valleys on the floor of the oceans caused by one plate in Earth's crust sliding under another.

desert: waterless areas on land. Mars is often considered a desert planet.

diameter: the thickness or width of something.

double stars: stars that circle each other.

eclipse: when one body crosses through the shadow of another. During a Solar Eclipse (eclipse of the Sun), parts of the Earth are in the shadow of the Moon as the Moon cuts right across the Sun and hides it for a period of time.

Einstein, Albert: a German-born US scientist. His many theories include those concerning unusual motions in a planet's orbit. He is perhaps the best known scientist of the twentieth century.

ellipse: an oval; the oval-shaped orbit a planet takes around the Sun.

evaporation (evaporates): the process that turns water into a vapor or gas.

Evening Star: the name by which Venus has long been known when it appears in the evening sky after sunset.

extinct: no longer living, or no longer active. Both the dinosaurs and inactive volcanoes are said to be extinct.

fault: a break in Earth's crust often found where plates come together.

fissure: a long, narrow crack, as in a rock or cliff face.

galaxy: any of the many large groupings of stars, gas, and dust that exist in the Universe. Our Galaxy is known as the Milky Way.

Galileo, Galilei: the Italian astronomer who in 1610 studied Venus through the first astronomical telescope.

gas giants: Jupiter, Saturn, Uranus, and Neptune; the farther planets from the Sun—not counting Pluto. They consist mostly of hydrogen and helium, rather than rock and metal.

gravity: the force that causes objects like the Earth and Moon to be attracted to one another.

"greenhouse effect": the phenomenon whereby heat entering a planet's atmosphere becomes trapped and continues to build up until the surface temperature of the planet is raised. It is thought to be responsible for Venus's being the hottest known place in the Solar system other than the Sun.

Hall, Asaph: an American astronomer who discovered the Martian satellites, or moons, called Phobos and Deimos.

helium: a light, colorless gas that makes up part of every star.

hydrogen: a colorless, odorless gas that is the simplest and lightest of the elements. Stars are three-quarters hydrogen.

Icarus: an asteroid that approaches the Sun even more closely than Mercury does; named after a mythological boy whose father made him wings of wax and feathers. He flew too close to the Sun and his wings melted, so he tumbled to the sea below.

Ice Ages: periods in the history of Earth that saw the movement of great ice glaciers across parts of the land surface of the planet.

ice cap: a cover of permanent ice at either or both ends of a planet. Mars has ice caps at both ends.

infrared radiation: "beneath the red" radiation. Infrared wavelengths are longer than red light wavelengths. Infrared radiation is invisible to the naked eye, but you can feel it as heat.

Ishtar Terra: the northernmost of Venus's two "continents," about the same size as the United States, named for the Babylonian goddess of love. All planetary features on Venus have female names. (See also *Aphrodite Terra*.)

Lucifer: a Latin name meaning "bringer of light," applied both to Venus as the Morning Star (because it rises before the Sun) and to the devil (as the most glorious of angels before his fall).

magnetic field: a field or area around a planet with a center of melted iron—such as Earth. The magnetic field is caused by the planet's rotation, which makes the melted iron in the planet's core swirl. As a result, the planet is like a huge magnet.

mantle: the hot, rocky matter that surrounds Earth's core.

Mariner 4: a space probe that in 1965 passed within 6,000 miles (9,600 km) of Mars and photographed the planet.

Mariner 9: a probe that reached Mars in 1971, orbited the planet, and took many photographs.

Mars: the god of war in ancient Roman mythology. The planet Mars is named for him.

mass: a quantity, or amount, of matter.

Morning Star: the name by which Venus has long been known when it appears in the morning sky before sunrise.

meteor: a tiny asteroid or meteoroid that has entered the Earth's atmosphere. Also, the bright streak of light made as the meteoroid enters or moves through the atmosphere.

meteorite: a meteoroid when it hits the Earth.

meteoroid: a lump of rock or metal drifting through space. Meteoroids can be as big as asteroids or as small as specks of dust.

moon: a large natural object that orbits around a planet.

natural satellites: another name for the moons that orbit planets.

nebula: a vast cloud of dust and gas in space.

nuclear fusion: the collision and combination of hydrogen atoms that produces helium.

Olympus Mons: a huge extinct volcano on Mars.

orbit: the path that one celestial object follows as it circles, or revolves, around another.

oxygen: the gas in Earth's atmosphere that makes human and animal life possible. Simple life forms changed carbon dioxide to oxygen as life evolved on Earth.

ozone layer: that part of our atmosphere that shields us from the Sun's dangerous ultraviolet rays.

Pangaea: the giant single continent that made up the land surface of Earth hundreds of millions of years ago.

phases: the periods when an object in space is partly or fully lit by the Sun. Like Earth's Moon, Mercury passes through phases as we watch it from Earth.

planet: one of the bodies that revolve around our Sun. Our Earth is one of the planets.

plates: sections of Earth's crust that are created by the movement of rock in Earth's mantle.

pole: either end of the axis around which a planet, moon, or star rotates.

probe: a craft that travels in space, photographing celestial bodies and even landing on some of them.

proto-: the earliest or first form of something. In this book, we talk about the young Sun as a "protostar" or "protosun," and about the early planets as "protoplanets."

pulsar: a star with all the mass of an ordinary large star but with its mass squeezed into a small ball. It sends out rapid pulses of light or electrical waves.

radiation: the spreading of heat, light, or other forms of energy by rays or waves.

radio telescope: an instrument that uses a radio receiver and antenna to both see into space and listen for messages from space.

radio waves: electromagnetic waves that can be detected by radio receiving equipment.

rotate: to turn or spin on an axis.

rocky planets: Mercury, Venus, Earth, and Mars; the planets closest to the Sun. They all have rock and metal at their centers.

satellite: a smaller body orbiting a larger body. The Moon is the Earth's *natural* satellite. Sputnik 1 and 2 were Earth's first *artificial* satellites.

Solar system: the Sun with the planets and all other bodies that orbit the Sun.

solar transit: the passing of a planet or other smaller astronomical body across the disk, or face, of the Sun.

solar wind: tiny particles that travel from the Sun's surface at a speed of about 250 miles (402 km) a second.

sulfuric acid: a corrosive liquid able to dissolve solid rock. It is found in Venus's atmosphere, making Venus one place where there is truly "acid rain."

Sun: our star and provider of the energy that makes life possible on Earth.

supernova: a red giant that has collapsed, heating its cool outer layers and causing explosions.

terraforming: making another world like Earth by giving it qualities that are, as far as we know, special to Earth, such as oxygen and water. *Terra* is Latin for "Earth."

twilight: the time at sunset when the Sun is below the horizon but there is still a little light left in the sky.

ultraviolet rays: a form of radiation that acts on photographic film and causes burning of your skin in sunshine.

Universe: everything that we know exists and that we believe may exist.

Valles Marineris: an enormous canyon on Mars.

Venus: the ancient Roman goddess of love. The planet was named after her because of its great beauty.

Viking 1 and 2: probes that actually landed on Mars and sent back information about the planet.

white dwarf: the small, white-hot body that remains when a star like our Sun collapses.

x-rays: a form of radiation that has a shorter wavelength than visible light and can thus pass through materials such as flesh and bones. The shorter its wavelength, the more easily an x-ray passes through a material.

Index

157